For Scott

Contents

Introduction. 1

ADVENT 7

what to expect when (you have no idea
what) you are expecting 9

leaning in 21

in your presents 33

CHRISTMAS. 45

making space 47

EPIPHANY 61

how to play. 63

LENT 79

the second week 81

getting it out. 95

out, damned spot! or the day i discovered
my oven knobs come off 105

CONTENTS

EASTER 117

but dairy cows already knew this 119

a sprinkling 135

PENTECOST 147

cultivation 149

ORDINARY TIME 167

the preacher's wife 169

on being nice 185

an evangelism tool 195

whirlybirds 205

Acknowledgments 219

Notes 223

grace in the maybe

Introduction

There was a time when I knew everything about God. I was young (you're not surprised) and relatively arrogant (now you're *really* not surprised). My team always won when we played Bible trivia games in my church youth group. I knew the stories of Jonah and Daniel and Saul like they were my own family stories; I could quote the most popular Bible verses; I memorized the order of the biblical books and could spell all their names. In the denomination my husband, Scott, was raised in, they had a name for people like me: Bible Quizzers. These Bible Quizzers would enter a districtwide competition. They would learn strategies about how to be the fastest student out of her chair in order to answer a question. They would order customized team shirts. Like marathon runners, these Quizzers would prep and train for months before the big day. I got really jealous when Scott told me about all of this; it could have been my chance for glory.

Somewhere along the way, I lost all that knowledge about God—or at least I began to realize how much there was to learn. Each day that I was a Christian seemed to be a step backward in understanding my faith. I started acknowledging the questions in my heart, began discussing those questions with friends and fellow saints—as those in the church are called, however undeserving the label may sometimes seem. And I discovered, after whining about how difficult all of this Christian stuff was, that the mystery of not knowing was also absolutely, undeniably wonderful.

It seems that some Christians never come to this realization, and they continue living lives of faith in which the answers about God, the universe, heaven, hell, and existence are abundantly and exceedingly clear. How nice for them. I don't mean to generalize about this type of person, but I know that the category exists because I come in contact with them often: on television, on blogs, on billboards. "God's Word is clear!" they often say. And somehow, their interpretations of the Bible are always, obviously the correct ones. Anyone else is wandering off into heretical territory, distorting the true Word of God for a lie.

> *i discovered that the mystery of not knowing was also absolutely, undeniably wonderful.*

I can't say that I envy people who view God this way, as they tend to miss out on the mystery and beauty of not knowing. This occurred to me recently during discussions I had with some Christians over Internet blogs and social media. Admittedly, this was a terrible idea, and I knew going in that trying to have any sort of honest discourse over hot-button issues via the Internet would land me nowhere but angry. I was right, but more, I was struck by how hollow the arguments sounded.

They were the same things, sometimes the very same *words,* I had said when I was a young Christian. Defensive, definitive, unrelenting, often arrogant.

A better Christian would probably forgive this sort of person. A better Christian would take Jesus' They-Know-Not-What-They-Do attitude, point out the goodness in the lives of even people who are irritatingly cocky and judgmental, add that their own sins are so great that they couldn't possibly fault somebody else for theirs. But I am only a mediocre Christian. I mess up quite often. I struggle with pride and self-loathing, sometimes at the same time. I go around saying, as Anne Lamott has joked that "I am not one of those Christians who is heavily into forgiveness—that I am one of the other kind."[1]

It is, perhaps, dangerous to begin a book on faith with this sort of confession. I should pretend, at least for a few pages, to be a person of substance and inner purity, someone who is nice most of the time, someone who, if painted during the Renaissance, would get a glowing halo. But this would only leave me feeling dishonest, and you, probably, pissed off. Either that or you would take some of the quotations from my book and make bumper stickers out of them.

Writing personal reflections—essays—has been a surprisingly natural fit for me in writing about God. The form is one that wanders, that claims no particularly special knowledge or authority; its grounding is in personal experience, and it seeks to make sense of things by asking questions and telling stories. This appeals to me precisely because, as Flannery O'Connor has noted, if a writer of faith "hopes to reveal mysteries, he will have to do it by describing truthfully what he sees from where he is."[2]

I'm happy to leave the podium to experts—men and women of faith who have studied hard, who have lived lives of compassion longer than I've been alive, and who probably could have beaten me at Bible Quizzing. I enjoy the amateur's seat. It seems natural to write about God from this perspective—a God whom I know but also one in whom I believe. I've never seen Him with physical eyes and certainly don't claim to always understand Him. Truth be told, even the greats—the specialists we've come to regard as experts about God—usually end up feeling like amateurs as they seek to explain God. The good ones, anyway.

The following reflections are organized around the liturgical church calendar. As a Protestant, I'd not grown up hearing much about such a calendar. Terms like *Lent* were reserved strictly for Catholics, and I possessed, for a variety of different reasons, a healthy amount of suspicion for anything not exclusively Protestant. Since then, I've noticed a longing for a tangible way to order my days, Protestant or not. Most Americans tend to order their lives in other ways: around the academic calendar or the fiscal year or basketball season. While all of these methods have their place, none of them really speaks to the deepest part of me, the part that desires a more spiritual focus, the part that desires to know God. The liturgical church calendar was adopted by the very early church, according to theologian Robert Webber, as a practice for focusing one's life on Jesus Christ; it is a way of remembering, year after year, his ministry, his death, his resurrection. Thousands of churches across the globe use passages from the lectionary in tandem to guide their holy day worship, and I like the idea of having this solidarity with worshippers I've never met and perhaps never will meet. More than that, it seems important that the way I order my life be in keeping with what I treasure most.

The first time I went fishing, my dad took my brother and me down to a very meager pond. Actually, it was more like a watering hole. Both Hutch and I had beginner poles—mine was blue and white and had a Snoopy emblazoned on it. Dad taught us how to bait the hooks, and we practiced for weeks the correct way to extend our arms behind us and release the line at just the right time to result in a perfect cast. We were bouncing with excitement, and I remember Dad cautioning us: "Fishing takes patience. We might not catch anything, all day, and that will be fine. We'll go out again."

The pebbly shoreline didn't deter us from running down to the water's edge, bending over at the waist to peer into the dark.

"I see one!" Hutch declared. He pointed excitedly at a zippy shape in the water, and my dad chuckled.

"Then let's get those lines in the water!"

I think mine was in first, and within a matter of seconds, I felt a tug at the end of my line. My eyes widened, and I looked immediately to my father for help.

"Give it a little tug," he said. "Not too much." Like that, he helped me lure in a glistening fish. My first one, wimpy in size but spunky in fight.

"Don't get used to that," Dad said. "They don't usually come that quickly."

But when Hutch cast, he got a similar response. We pulled in fish after fish that morning, after a while not even bothering to bait the line; they'd bite whether we tempted them or not. The pond was teeming with fish.

It was an anomaly, to be sure. Since that day, I've never had a fishing experience quite like it, even though we went back to that same pond later to try again. Most of my expeditions since have involved few glimpses of actual fish. Was it simply the time of year that made the catch so plentiful? Or maybe the pond had been recently restocked? Some would say we were just lucky, that the season and the weather conditions and the water-to-algae ratio and the stars all aligned and we just happened to be at the right place at the right time. Still others would insist that I'm remembering it wrong. I'll never know the truth.

the surprise might be exactly what makes it worthwhile.

An experienced fisherman will tell you that, no matter how good you are, you will not always catch fish like this. An experienced fisherman will tell you that fishing is a lesson in patience, in being prepared, in learning the circumstances and locations and times most conducive to catching fish, and in being there. But he will also tell you that there's an element of pure surprise about it all. The surprise might be exactly what makes it worthwhile.

Advent

what to expect when
(you have no idea what)
you are expecting

❧

Some days, especially in early spring and late fall, the wind in Kansas can't decide on a direction. It whips around tall grasses, girls' skirts, and strands of hair, flings them skyward and lets go just as fast, dances with dried leaves and felled blossoms, skips across dirt and concrete. If it's warm outside, I love these days. Perhaps it comes from growing up near the Pacific Ocean, where wind belongs to the coastlines and smells like water, even if you're an hour's drive from the sea. Perhaps it is just the feel of moving air against bare skin, the unfathomable idea that that same air was miles away only moments before.

Most of my friends find this love for the wind odd; they fear tornadoes and bad hair days, and they hate not being able to read their newspapers outside. They like days that are still, and I can't blame them. The wind mixes things up, gets dirt in your eyes, makes your umbrella flip inside out, causes you to yank at the bottom of your dress so you don't unintentionally flash passersby. It is inconvenient, but for me, it is powerful and alive. It makes me think of God and the stories that parents tell their children about how God is in the weather: crying when it rains, smiling through miles of sky in rays of sunshine, moving the clouds around like pieces of a jigsaw puzzle. In the wind, He must be whispering down to us, reminding us that He is out there, powerful, unpredictable, profoundly and utterly mysterious.

When I was pregnant with my first child, the term *expecting* never really sat well with me; it may have even added to the morning sickness.

"Just call me pregnant," I told people, "or maybe full with child." Those descriptions seemed more apt. I would even rather have been referred to as having a bun in the oven, and because I am a writer and ardent hater of clichés, that should tell you something. The term *expecting* suggests to me a sort of certainty or knowledge about what is coming, and since this was my first bun in said oven, I had little of either.

I suppose there are a few things I expected, like having to buy bigger pants, but most of the time I felt ill prepared to expect anything at all. The only baby books I had in my house were borrowed because purchasing one—the right one—seemed too daunting. (The sole exception was the newest edition of *Baby Bargains*, which was not frightening because it involves only shopping.) On the rare occasion that I did crack open one of those borrowed books, I got only as far as how big the kid was that week, what sort of fruit or vegetable was comparable to it in size. When the author started getting too specific, describing things like how developed the baby's lungs are, for instance, I freaked out and moved on to *Martha Stewart Living*. Keeping hydrangeas alive seemed much simpler than building lungs, even though I had killed the last two plants I owned before the season was over.

Perhaps the overwhelming nature of what it means to be carrying a child plunged me into a state of denial. It was strange, for instance, to call what used to be my stomach—or sometimes, when I am in a Pilates phase, my abs—a "belly." (As far as I know, only Santa Claus, beer guzzlers, and pregnant women have bellies.) Little bits of change at a time are all I can handle. That's why, when the sonogram technician asked my husband, Scott, and me if we'd like to know the sex of the baby, I said no. We asked, instead, that she write it down and put it in a sealed envelope. She did, and that envelope was then tucked away in a safe place. Contrary to my dad's belief that I peeked and was just refusing to tell anybody, I wasn't even tempted to look. Knowing there would be a little human around in just a few months, an actual living, breathing, crying, growing-up human, was enough information for me at that point. I was still struggling with the big pants.

i suppose there are a few things i expected, like having to buy bigger pants, but most of the time i felt ill prepared to expect anything.

Some women try to tell you what to expect. In fact, once your belly is of the size that even strangers feel comfortable in asking your due date, anyone who answers to the name "mom" will give you advice, solicited or not, on how to get rid of morning sickness, what kind of stroller works best on rough terrain, and how to deal with nipple chafing. They want to know all about your birth plan, if you are getting the epidural, and whether or not you want to breast-feed. Then, they will offer their opinions regarding (usually) why you are wrong. Although I can acknowledge their good intentions, I mostly ignored their advice.

My birth plan, at that point, was dreadfully incomplete anyway. The work sheet my midwife gave me asked questions ranging from "When (if ever) would you like your health care professional to instigate a C-section?" to "Would you like background music?" and "What sort of lighting is most comfortable for you?" Pardon me for being unable to decide if I'd like James Taylor's "How Sweet It Is (to Be Loved by You)" or Metallica's "Enter Sandman" playing while I'm pushing, groaning, and sweating out a tiny person. I just didn't know.

who expects preposterous?

It really makes me feel for the Virgin Mary when I think about all the news she got at once: (1) You're pregnant; (2) He's the Son of God; (3) I know you haven't had sex yet. We're calling you "Immaculate"; (4) His name will be Jesus, which means "God with Us"; and (5) You'll have to buy bigger pants.

It seems ironic to me that Advent, the first season of the church calendar, the season celebrating the events leading up to Christ's birth, is a time of expectation. What, exactly, was Mary to expect? What was Israel to expect? They had been promised a conquering Savior—and now here was this kid. This *kid,* born to a virgin, destined to die a ridiculous death on a cross before his thirty-fifth birthday. It was preposterous. It *is* preposterous. Who expects preposterous?

The acceptance of the preposterous, the irrational, the unexplainable, the unexpected, shows up frequently in the Bible: when Abraham and Sarah are told to expect a child in the (very) late years of their lives, or when Joseph is sent to prison after being promised that he will be made a leader, or when Saul, a well-known persecutor of Jews, becomes a convert and eventually a major contributor to the New Testament.

It's difficult to name the baffling and the uncertain as part of the Christian experience, especially when so much of American fundamentalism is based upon being absolutely certain of its tenets of faith. I remember seeing a T-shirt in a Christian-bookstore catalog many years ago that read: "God said it. I believe it. That settles it." I wanted that shirt. I cut the picture out of the catalog and hung it up on my bulletin board with other inspirational phrases and verses. It was such a wonderful mantra: confident, bold, assured. It meant that I knew exactly what I was doing in this world, and that is quite a feat to have accomplished by high school. I lived that way, too. I told other people, like my Mormon prom date, that they were going to hell if they didn't change their ways. I argued with my biology teacher about coming from monkeys. I prayed at the flagpole that American schools wouldn't continue to keep God out of the classroom. I felt 100 percent sure that I was right. After all, God said it.

As years went by, the "it" that God said began to feel a bit murkier. After all, God didn't really say anything specific about Mormons or monkeys or flagpoles. I started wondering, in the smallest, darkest parts of my mind and heart, whether I was right to have believed it and settled it so easily. I couldn't pretend that God was speaking to me audibly, giving me insight into exactly who could be expected in heaven and how they were formed and created without the help of evolution or school boards. He was only whispering.

From the beginning of time, when the waters covered the great expanse of the earth, God has been whispering:

> *And the earth was waste and void;*
> *and darkness was upon the face of the deep:*
> *and the RUACH of God moved upon the face of the*
> *   waters.*[1]

The Hebrew word *ruach* is used more than 375 times in the Bible, beginning with the reference in Genesis 1:2. Its root means "moving air," whether in the form of breath, storm winds, or gentle breezes, and it is usually translated in English as "wind." *Ruach* is used when God breathes first life into Adam, when he separates the Red Sea so Moses and the Israelites can pass safely through, and when Jesus breathes his last on the cross. Breath is tied closely to a person's creation of words, so it's not too much of a jump to say that *ruach,* in each of these references, might also indicate the state of God's heart and mind. It is God's presence, felt and witnessed in winds great enough to separate a sea and weak enough to be expelled as one's last gasp as he suffocates during crucifixion.

• • •

My friend Maria, who was pregnant the same time I was, used to get mad at me because my breasts weren't expanding as rapidly as hers. I was just as mad. She had to buy two new bras within the first couple months of her pregnancy, while I was just beginning to fill out my old one. My pregnant breasts were as dainty as my regular breasts, and my delusions of bountiful cleavage—even cleavage that lasted only a few months—rapidly faded. As we compared things like who had worse morning sickness, whose lower back hurt more, and whose belly button looked less like an actual belly button, we both ended up feeling as though we'd gotten the short end of the pregnancy stick. We shouldn't have subjected ourselves to these endless comparisons, but all I could expect of pregnancy was what I had seen happen to other women who were, or who had been, pregnant. This isn't really expectation. Especially considering that every book I read or woman I spoke to summed it up this way: every woman is different.

Although I prepared for pregnancy by reading the books, filling out birth-plan work sheets, comparing my belly button to anyone else's who would let me, I couldn't know how to explain or imagine the feel of tiny fists and elbows nudging me from inside my abdomen. And I couldn't even begin to understand how it would feel to hold my son or daughter for the first time. My expectations of motherhood were astoundingly small and shortsighted, but who could blame me? How could I possibly expect what was in store?

"Where there is doubt, faith has its reason for being,"[2] writes Daniel Taylor in *The Myth of Certainty*. "Clearly faith is not

needed where certainty supposedly exists, but only in situa-
tions where doubt is possible, even present." When I read this
in college, an almost physical sense of relief came over me. I
highlighted the sentence, along with most of the other sentences on the page, and went to bed happy that I didn't have
to decide anymore whether any of my former prom dates or
the indigenous, un-churched people of the Australian outback
would go to heaven. I didn't even have to be constantly certain
that there is a God.

Since then, doubt has been more a solidification of my
faith than a hindrance to it. It seems only logical that a God—a
God—would far surpass any of my expectations about who
He is and how He should behave. If He wants to be preposterous, who am I to tell Him otherwise?

I have never felt God's presence more completely than I
did at the very end of my labor. The baby had crowned (and
apparently wanted to stay in that uncomfortable position longer than I'd have liked), and I breathed deeply in the short
times between contractions.

In the back of my mind, I remembered stories of other
women's labors I'd heard of or seen. Most of them were on
television sitcoms, where women cursed at their husbands for
getting them into "this mess" and screamed at the tops of their
lungs because some intern had flubbed the epidural. Labor
was not as frightening for me. In fact, while it wasn't a feeling
I was anxious to repeat when my second child came along,
labor was the best kind of pain because it was not just pain,
but work.

"That's right," my midwife said, "just breathe that baby

out." This was one of Debbie's favorite pieces of encouragement. Though it was mildly offensive to my prelabor self who was certain, after being indoctrinated by enough *Friends* episodes, that I could expect dramatic pain during (and perfect makeup and hair after) the labor. But the phrase soothed me in the end stages of giving birth. Of course, calling the moaning and puffing I was doing "breathing" is a bit liberal, but the methodic ins and outs of breath did help the baby down the birth canal. Soon, the same tiny fists and elbows I'd felt for months inside me emerged, brand-new, and I felt each one give a final prod before the midwife laid a gasping baby boy on my naked chest. I could feel his heartbeat on mine; both of them were fast with effort, relief, delight.

doubt has been more a solidification of my faith than a hindrance to it.

That moment must be similar to the first few seconds of a free fall, or maybe how Mozart felt when he finished a particularly astonishing sonata: *I can't believe I just did that.* The nurses smiled, massaged the blood into his limbs, and worked quickly to suction the gunk out of his air passages so he could breathe.

I've heard before that in ancient times, very devout men and women respected the word *Yahweh,* the name of the Lord, so deeply that they did not speak it or write it; they chose instead a good substitute like *Elohim* or *Adonai.* I've also heard that those who needed to write it did a cleansing ritual every time they did. (I did not cleanse just then, I confess.) I've reminded myself of this serious sacredness whenever I use God's name in an under-my-breath, offhand way. Although

I am impressed by this respect for God's holiness, I probably will never understand it well enough to emulate it. I'm not even sure what the cleansing entailed or if there was, perhaps, a limit on the number of times you could physically write it. But Franciscan priest Richard Rohr notes that the Hebrew spelling of God's name, YHVH, is *literally* an unspeakable word for the Jewish people. He writes: "Formally the word was not spoken at all, but *breathed*! Many are convinced that its correct pronunciation is an attempt to replicate and imitate the very sound of inhalation and exhalation. The one thing we do every moment of our lives is therefore to speak the name of God."[3] And this I can understand, especially now, after hearing Miles's voice for the first time, in an inhalation and wail that resonated and bounced off the walls of the birthing room. It was pure magic, and the closest I have come to audibly hearing God.

Even as I write this, I realize how hopeless it is to attempt to describe the indescribable. It makes me feel like turning in my laptop for good—just get out of this whole writing debacle before people realize what a hack I am. But my complete inadequacy in describing my son's birth also reconvinces me of God's presence, because there must be something out there bigger than me, than us, if there are moments like these. And there are. All the time. Inordinate surprises that, most often, are wrapped up in so much love that we wonder where it all came from.

I used to know a little boy named Jackson who loved to play in the backyard, but never near a big, scary red bush that dominated one side of it. Although he wanted nothing to do with the bush and would cry if I tried to carry him near it, he did not completely avoid it. Instead, he would orbit it at a distance he'd deemed "safe." One day, out of bravery or perhaps boredom, he picked up a seed pod that had dropped from a nearby tree, approached the bush, and threw it into the bush's dark center. Then he waited. His body tense, his face drawn and serious, he could have been gazing down at an army of thousands, daring them to approach. Of course, the bush swallowed up the pod and spat nothing back at the little warrior.

Jackson felt encouraged by the victory and made throwing the prickly seed pods part of his daily routine. It was his encounter with mystery. I still smile at his fascination with the unknown depths of the bush, the way he'd finally given up being afraid but still hadn't lost the curious wonder regarding that which he didn't understand.

Perhaps expectation is as much about opening ourselves up to surprise as it is about knowing, or even preparing for, what's next. As Mary waited for the birth of her son, I'm sure she was scared—no matter how many visits she got from explanatory angels. There probably was no book titled *Mothering the Christ Child for Dummies,* so she had to trust God even when He did wonky things like using a really bright star as a GPS system. But it all seemed to work out fine for her.

It's easier for me to imagine God's power on windy days, and I'll often find myself breathing his name, in and out, as I listen for whatever it is he might be whispering. Usually, I have no idea, but even that has become less a means of frustration and more a means of grace. It seems that we all try to harness the wind in small ways—in hair dryers and leaf blowers and pellet guns. These devices give us a feeling of power for a moment, the ability to put hair and leaves and tin-can targets in their places. Then we turn them off, and even that fragment of the wind is no longer under our control. We leave it up to God again, as we must.

I like it better that way. I much prefer the wind in quantities and strengths larger than the blow-dryer; but I think, on some level, everyone does. How else do you explain the popularity of things like the convertible, the Harley-Davidson, the roller coaster, the bungee jump? The wind whips at us as we barrel along, taking us straight on, hitting us on our faces, giving us a feeling of freedom that is both totally surprising and something we've all somehow come to expect.

leaning in

"Merry frickin' Christmas," I said. My friend AnneMarie was staring at the ceiling of the badly wallpapered hotel room.

"I don't want to do anything," she said. "Let's just stay in bed."

"We should go see some stuff," I said.

"Yeah, we should."

"We should go to church."

"Yeah, we should."

"I'll set the alarm."

"Okay."

We had arrived in Brussels on Christmas Eve, the wind and sleety-snow outside relentless and our bare faces stuck into half smiles, half grimaces. We had already spent a few days traveling through Holland and on into Belgium. Although the trip was not without mishaps (we spent fifteen minutes trying to withdraw money from a parking meter one day), AnneMarie and I finally felt confident that we could navigate these unfamiliar cities without too much trouble.

"Okay, where's this street we're looking for?" I asked. We leaned in toward the tiny map in our battered copy of *Let's Go: Europe* and found our hostel. We glanced up at the name on the street sign nearest us. The hostel was supposed to be right here, but the streets didn't match.

"We can do this," I said. The straps of my backpack, which was filled almost to bursting with heavy winter clothes, were carving indentations on my shoulders. I knew I should have felt more excited to be here, but all I could muster up was the desire to locate, in real, concrete terms, one damn street from the travel guide.

After a half hour of struggling to decipher the charades of Belgians attempting to be helpful, we decided to try the bus. That idea only served to tangle us up more, but we found a place to buy a larger map.

"Are we sure we're in Brussels?" AnneMarie asked. Our faces were now in full grimace.

I looked up at tall stone buildings, each one intricately carved and covered in bas-relief. It looked like Brussels.

We sat down on a bench in front of an enormous museum that was set high above dozens of rows of stone steps. Neither of us cared much that the museum was closed, that we'd probably never get a glimpse of the hundreds of treasures on display there. We only wanted a place to lie down and get out of the cold Belgian air. We readjusted scarves and hats and tried to summon some of the enthusiasm we had when, two weeks prior, we'd begun our backpacking trip. Because it was Christmas Eve, though, we were both quietly missing the traditions that were taking place at home—the traditions that seemed easy enough to miss months before when we were purchasing our plane tickets. The last time I spoke with my dad on the phone, he'd made sure to remind me how selfish my decision to "miss Christmas" had been. I'd made sure to ignore him. Only now his voice kept coming back.

Just as we began to pull on our backpacks again, we saw a man in dark clothes run out from behind a museum pillar and grab what looked to be a very expensive camera from a tourist who was small and old and unable to chase the thief. He cried out in a language we didn't understand, but nobody seemed to be listening. He was far away, but we could see the anguish in the way he flailed his arms and staggered a few steps after the thief. AnneMarie and I both stood up, but we were staircases away from being able to help. We watched as the old tourist dropped his face into his hands, alone. We felt powerless and discouraged at this show of heartlessness on the celebration of the eve of Christ's birth. This part of the trip, so far, was not shaping up well. We continued our journey to the hostel in relative silence, both of us wishing we were back home baking cookies or complaining about how there was nothing to do in our hometown.

he'd made sure to remind me how selfish my decision to "miss christmas" had been. i'd made sure to ignore him.

Then AnneMarie stepped into a half-frozen puddle of water. Her left pant leg was wet up to the knee.

"I hate Brussels," she said. But we had finally made it to the hostel.

• • •

"We are closed for Christmas," the hostel guy said, opening the door just a crack to address our incessant knocking. I should have been pregnant on a donkey.

Traditionally, Christmas is the culmination of the Christian season of Advent. The word *Advent* means "coming" or "arrival," so Christians are supposed to practice the posture of waiting on the birth of the Christ child. This is a somewhat weird thing to do, considering that the Christ child was born quite a while ago, and we are usually not inclined to wait for things that have already happened. For instance, no one is waiting anymore for *Rocky II* to come out. It just doesn't make a whole lot of sense. Still, my church has taught me that the act of waiting is an important thing to practice, whether it makes sense or not.

The other thing that we are supposed to be waiting for during Advent is Christ's *second* coming. This is also quite mysterious, because Jesus said that no one will ever expect the day or the hour he decides to come again. My friend Emily, when she was very little, was terrified of the second coming of Christ, so she would sit on her front porch, eyes slammed shut, and repeat, "I'm expecting it, I'm expecting it, I'm expecting it." She was sure that Christ, after hearing that, would have to stay put, and she would have the chance someday to get married and go to prom—maybe not in that order. She has always been good at finding loopholes.

Waiting for Christ's birth and his second coming concurrently can be a bit tricky, especially because God has always said that He isn't done yet. Some theologians call this "the time between the times." My husband, Scott, went to seminary, so he spent many years thinking and reading specifically about God. He says one idea that might help us understand the tension between waiting on Christ's birth and waiting on Christ's second coming is *eschatology*. Eschatology is the study of last things and can highlight the complicated balance of living in *this* part of the story while anticipating the end of the story, like people who read the last page of a Stephen King novel before they are even done with the first chapter and then pretend they'd had everything figured out the whole time. We know how things are supposed to be because Jesus talked all about it (even though he was sort of cryptic), yet we can't experience it in its fullness yet. Instead, we have to deal with what we've got in chapter six. That means that we must put up with not really understanding why bad things happen to good people, or why the tulips in the yard only bloom for a few

that means that we must put up with not really understanding why bad things happen to good people, or why the tulips in the yard only bloom for a few days.

days (and those days usually happen when you are in line at the DMV or visiting your grandmother in Cincinnati) and then die until that same time next year, or why innocent children are sometimes hurt because people who are supposed to be grown up and mature decide to kill each other over land or power or gas prices.

In essence, we are sort of stuck in this tension-ridden period of limbo. The game limbo is, indeed, a good way to describe how awkward this period is—when half of your body is on one side of the stick and half of your body is on the other side and all the blood is rushing to your face.

After being denied room at the hostel, we figured that a hotel was our only option. We got on the train and were dropped off on the edge of the city at the very last train stop—lost again. If we'd had any confidence that we'd be able to find the airport successfully, we probably would have flown home. As it was, we boarded the train back to the city and put all of our college-educated wits to finding shelter.

Finally, we arrived at a quaint little hotel that was marked with only two dollar signs in our travel guide: Hotel Pacific. It seemed at once affordable and reminiscent of California's ocean and home. It was a narrow building that went up and up, and when we entered, we nearly bumped into the reception desk. The posters of famous landmarks were jaundiced and had numerous pinpricks at their edges, the furniture was heavy with years and paperwork, and the wallpaper looked like what Carol Brady would have chosen if she'd married Louis XIV and had gotten to decorate Versailles all by herself. Everything around us had survived since the 1970s. The couple who ran the place looked even older, like they had memorized the senior menu in 1970. But they were kind. They gave us a room, which was up rickety steps and around lots of tight corners, but clean and quiet.

It was our own little Bethlehem stable, and we were thankful for the kindness.

• • •

I decided that the only thing that could begin to heal my battered spirit and body was a shower. I was right, but only for a moment. Many things are healing, I've found, but only for a moment: massages, coffee, sore-throat spray, vodka, jokes at other people's expense, shopping, and now, showers. The water was wonderful and made the bathroom into a European spa with its hotness and steam. It made trails down the backs of my travel-weary calves. I was so tired that I forgot my shower shoes and, for once, didn't care that I might contract athlete's foot.

But drying off . . .

Back in the States, before the backpacking began, AnneMarie had lectured me on the importance of keeping my pack light. Since she was the one who always remembered to send birthday cards on time and she had consulted both the *Blue Book* and *Consumer Reports* before buying her first car, I listened to her about stuff like this.

"You don't want to be hauling a whole bunch of crap all over Europe," she'd said.

So I did my best to pack light. I brought only one shade of eye shadow, for instance. And instead of bringing a regular sort of towel, I bought the special "travel towel" that they sell for camping at a campground in Yosemite, or maybe in the wilderness of the arctic tundra. The towel was Dodger blue, stiff, scratchy, and expensive. I'd bought it at the last minute, so I didn't even launder the thing, just threw it into the backpack and trusted that AnneMarie was right.

When I unfolded it for the first time thousands of miles from home, I realized that the towel that seemed so tiny all folded up was actually the size of a bedsheet. And it was stiff, like the rough side of a very large sponge. My dry skin was irritated and red when I finally got back to the room—and I was only half dry.

I snapped. I threw the towel into our little sink and turned the water on full blast, hoping that this faux-laundering would soften the towel's hard edges so I would never have to endure the scratchiness again. What ended up happening, though, was that the towel did what it was made to do: it soaked up a lot of water. It was heavy, sopping, and cold when I was done with it, and I had no good place to hang it up. I draped the towel over the tiny sink and mentally resigned myself to drying off with napkins stolen from McDonald's for the rest of our time in Brussels. Then I yelled at AnneMarie for suggesting I buy the towel at all. We went to the grocery store angry at each other and picked up a makeshift Christmas dinner.

It probably wasn't the stick of sausage, bag of provolone, and box of crackers that made us frustrated. We ate together but were lonely nonetheless. Since we had no source of refrigeration, we left the rest of the food on the windowsill for the night and trusted the chill to keep the meat cold.

"Never will I leave you," Christ promised. "And never will you have to undergo a cold, miserable, lonely, scratchy Christmas." Perhaps I'm remembering that last part wrong. But sometimes, I wish he'd included the last part. Sometimes, I want things to go well, and I want people to like me, and I want those who are sick to always get better. But Jesus never said those things, and that is part of living between the comings, I suppose.

My former pastor, Mindy, says that God has a sort of problem in that He is quite holy and must preserve His holiness, but at the same time, He has connected himself to a sinful people. There is bound to be some tension there. God came down to earth amid the sinful humanity that He loved so much that He couldn't stop reaching, and He gave us a reason to hope again. Pastor Mindy says that we celebrate Christmas because it was the day the whole world changed. *Emmanuel: God with us.*

There is a sculpture I saw long ago at the Tate Modern in London. I did not write down the name of the sculptor, but the image has stayed with me all of these years. The piece was called *Tension,* and it looked a little like a crescent moon flipped on its back. The two points, however, were so near each other that I had to get quite close to the sculpture to see that they were not, in fact, touching, only leaning vehemently toward each other. It was beautiful and aching, like the moment before a first kiss.

When the alarm went off for the second time on Christmas morning, neither AnneMarie nor I was in better spirits. Still, since it was Christmas and since we were in Europe and therefore required to get out of bed and see things, we got ready to go to church. My towel was still sopping wet on the sink.

it was beautiful and aching, like the moment before a first kiss.

We arrived at the cathedral late, and the service was already in session. We quietly sat down at a pew in the back and listened to the priest, who was reciting scripture in Latin. Had I been home, the pastor at my parents' church would have been reading from some Christian children's story, as was his tradition. My brother and I would be scratching the wax from the candles the church staff would have handed out for the culmination of the service, in which "Silent Night" would be sung, a capella, by the congregation. My mother would be pleading with her eyes for us to stop messing around and pay attention. None of that happened to me here, though, where AnneMarie and I sat up straight and respectfully in the wooden pew and did our best to mimic the rest of the congregation when the movement of the service shifted.

Something about the melodically monotonous string of Latin was so quieting to us both that it surprised me. And the cathedral's ceiling, which stretched up and on forever like Kansas skies, was beautiful after the chaotic bustle of street maps, museum crowds, and train stations. God was there, too, somewhere in all that air.

i asked god to take all of that hatred out of me. and i asked him to dry my towel.

I thought about the day before and the effort it took to get here, where my feet and my heart were finally warm. I thought about the man who was stealing cameras on Christmas Eve, and I wondered if he had a place to be today. I wondered if I would give him a place if I had one; I knew I probably wouldn't. I probably would have just kept wondering whether the cameras he stole had other people's honeymoon pictures on them or maybe the birth of a grandchild. I asked God to take all of that hatred out of me, to remind me that love is always bigger than bitterness. And I asked Him to dry my towel.

That was the first time that Christmas Day that I'd felt peace, and for a moment I sort of sensed what it was like to wait in an Advent sort of way. I had no idea what the man in the pulpit was saying, nor had I lived any of my life with the people surrounding me in the pews, but here was family. If this little glimpse of God could somehow be translated into a whole life experience, maybe that would come close to looking like the last page. *Emmanuel: God with us.*

The last thing we did that night was to huddle inside a phone booth and call home.

My mom reminisced, letting me know that she had been to Brussels, too, when she was about my age, and had eaten lots of chocolate here. This was strangely comforting, to have a shared experience with my mother, whose days of being adventurous and young still seemed like undeveloped photographs to me. It was like getting to know her as a friend.

I talked to my dad next, who forgave me (for the day at least) for deserting the family, and he told me he loved me. I treasure up the times when my dad says "I love you," because he is not the type to say it every time he hangs up the phone, or even every time I leave for college. It isn't that he never says it; it is only that he chooses his moments carefully. I have a collection of notes on my refrigerator door that say those words in big Dad-scrawled letters. They are precious because they are rare.

In many ways, the love of Christ is most easily recognizable to me in small moments, in unexpected gestures of goodness and love. It is mysterious and just a glimpse, but it is there. It is so close you have to lean in to make sure it's still a part of this world and not quite the next.

"I dry your blanket," the old woman said, ushering us in as we returned for the evening. She handed me the enormous Dodger-blue towel. It was soft and welcoming to the touch.

in your presents

Standing in a line at a Kohl's department store at six-thirty in the morning was the first time I realized that I hated Christmas. I was a teenager when I heard my mom voice that same sentiment, but I thought she was exaggerating. I have since changed my opinion. This particular line wrapped from the front cash registers past the red display cases where everything was five dollars and the Perfect Gift—a manicure set, an automotive emergency set, a razor set, an iPod attachment set . . . the line went past the Ladies' Apparel and snaked around the toys, which were all glorified advertisements for one Disney movie or another. Now I was staring a bit glassy-eyed at a sign that read EARLY BIRD DOOR-BUSTER SPECIAL. I imagined us as a flock of angry—but early—bluebirds pecking through the thick glass of the motorized front doors of Kohl's to get to the prize: another generic sweater, this time made of some sort of shiny synthetic fabric—perfect for nesting.

"Oh, a reflective sweater. It will be useful if I ever decide to direct small-plane landings," I can imagine my mom saying. Still, I picked one up in red.

The people around me were mostly of two sorts. There

were ones who wandered aimlessly down the aisles, still wearing pajama tops under jean jackets in a halfhearted attempt at being presentable. Those people, like me, had hair that indicated precisely which sides of their heads were smashed onto their pillows only an hour ago. The other type looked as if they'd had amphetamines injected into their systems. These people usually came in teams of two and had checklists and coupons and maps of the store. They were unstoppable, and I quickly realized it was best to stay out of their way. After all, they had been camping out at the store's entrance since four A.M. in the freezing sleet.

the only silver lining i could see was that i at least had something to wrap up for each member of the family.

The thing that united these two groups of shoppers was one goal: to get the Christmas shopping done early—especially so you can brag to all of your more pathetic friends who leave it to the last minute every season. (Well, maybe that last part was just *my* goal. I've been in the "pathetic friend" category more than I'd care to admit.) Even the stuff I'd picked up that morning seemed desultory at best. The only silver lining I could see was that I at least had something to wrap up for each member of the family—even if it was only a five-dollar manicure set.

I worked retail for one year at an Ann Taylor store. Right before the Christmas season, we had our annual Black Friday meeting. This is when employees from all the regional stores get together to eat too many cookies and devise a game plan for the holidays, and especially for that most manic day of the year, the day after Thanksgiving. The goal of the meeting was twofold: (1) to figure out how to survive Black Friday without being fired for cussing out the defenseless old woman who destroyed the stack of cardigans you've just finished folding for the seventh time (the old battle-ax); and (2) to learn how to effectively seduce people into buying cashmere even when you're pretty sure they can only afford cotton. That meeting alone convinced me that I wasn't cut out for retail sales, but my husband and I needed the money, so I had to stick it out for the season. It constantly amazes me what some people will do for money.

The term *Black Friday,* if you have never held a retail sales position, seems a bit of an overstatement. *Could it really be that bad?* you may ask yourself. But when you watch a woman walk out of the dressing room with the silhouette of a hanger embedded under her pants near her rear end, you become a bit more convinced that it could be. Or when a sleep-deprived, well-dressed woman wants the last deeply discounted black cashmere sweater in size medium, and she leaves no display table untouched, no dressing room unthrashed, no salesperson unharassed in her quest to find the sweater. (She will usually succeed, then give the sweater to her daughter-in-law, who will, inevitably, return said sweater to the same salesperson the day after Christmas.) Then you *really* begin to wonder. Or when someone tries to return hiking boots from a decade ago that have clearly been used to go alligator hunting in the Florida wetlands ("But they were a gift. And they still have their tags attached," she insists). Yes, you're now sure; it really is that bad.

• • •

Our whole concept of gift giving is somewhat skewed when each member of the family writes out a list—as detailed as possible, please—and distributes it to all other members of the family so they know what to purchase and wrap. Somehow, the list becomes one more of demands than of wishes, and we stop just short of handing out itemized bills to our relatives, complete with SKU numbers and a place for credit card information.

My friend Nick's Catholic mother used to tell him that the reason their family gave Christmas presents was because, on a night long ago, three wise kings brought the baby Jesus frankincense and myrrh. She said she was just continuing the tradition. Nick thought about this for a while and began wondering if the next year, when the baby Jesus was celebrating his first birthday, the wise kings decided to return with a bigger bottle of myrrh or some Frankincense 6.0. He suspected they didn't, and decided not to ask his mother about it. Instead, he nodded in agreement.

The most notorious gift giver in America is, by far, the fat man with the distinctive laugh and the posse of small, pointy-eared men with a knack for building stuff. Most people are generally aware that Santa Claus is a modernized, commercialized version of a fourth-century saint named Nicholas. Very few people, however, seem to know his story. In fact, there is very little we know for sure about Saint Nicholas. He left behind no writings of his own, so what has been passed down is a mixture of fact, folklore, and a little embellishment for good measure.

The most famous story is of a man who lost all his money and couldn't afford dowries for his three daughters. Because the daughters were unmarriageable and, well, women, most people figured they would turn to prostitution in order to survive. Upon hearing this story, Saint Nicholas sneaked over to the house one night and threw a bag of gold through an open window. (Or, if you are really romantic, down the chimney.) He occasionally did things like this, using money he'd inherited from his parents' deaths for works of charity; and he always did it in secret, making sure to slink away

the word more *is already a cultural disease, and now it has crept into and distorted our understanding of generosity.*

before anyone had the chance to know who their benefactor was. He preferred it this way. Saint Nicholas then came back to the same house the next week (some historians say the next year) to hide another bag of gold for the second daughter. But by the third time, the father had caught on. He stayed awake to find out who was leaving them all that money. (Oh, come on, wouldn't you?) When he found out it was Saint Nicholas, he told everyone who would listen. Saint Nicholas became known as the patron saint of children and gift giving, among other random things including sailors and pawnbrokers, but that is for a different essay.

December 6 is noted on Catholic calendars as the Feast of Saint Nicholas, and it usually falls within the first week of Advent. In many European countries, the Feast is an even greater celebration than Christmas. It is a day to remember the saint's dedication to giving to those who really needed it, and doing it in a way that drew as little attention to himself as possible.

Well, suffice it to say that the connection between the Saint and the Santa is a loose one. The American Santa was actually adapted mostly from the Dutch *Sinterklaas,* who was based on, but already a step removed from, ol' Saint Nick. Santa's noble beginnings, however far away they may be, sound much more enticing than the list-checking distributor we know today as "the patron saint of shopping till you drop"—as writer Robert Niebuhr calls him. The exhaustion that phrase insinuates used to be hyperbole—but not anymore. Not when you hear about people being trampled to death all over the nation as shoppers race toward "door-crasher" specials and limited deals. Shopping has become a winner-take-all bloodsport.

Recently, one of the megamarts was selling itself by running a commercial that said: "The more you save, the more Christmas you can give." This seems to hit on the addictive selfishness that giving gifts sometimes becomes. The word *more* is already a cultural disease, and now it has crept into and distorted our understanding of generosity. Perhaps a departure from a "more"-obsessed culture is the best reason to return to a more Saint Nicholasish type of giving.

While rifling through a catalog from World Vision last year, I learned that, instead of purchasing that new PlayStation people were standing in Kohl's lines for, you could purchase a goat (or, if you are a little strapped for cash, one-fifth of a goat) for a family that isn't very well fed. I wondered if Saint Nicholas would have bought a goat. Probably so, I thought. Goats seem somehow in line with the keeping-people-out-of-prostitution gig. Then I wondered if the megamart would have had a better price on one?

Our church sponsored a program a few years ago called Operation Christmas Child. (Contrary to what its name evokes, it is not related in any way to any war.) The goal of this program was to remind us of the importance of giving to the poor and to help us practice that discipline in small ways, to help us learn to give as Saint Nicholas had. They showed an introductory video that explained how each family should go to the store and buy things that would be terrible presents if you gave them to your own children but wonderful presents for someone in Kenya or Sudan: toothbrushes, socks, maybe a comb. You would also throw in a toy or two, because even third-world children like to take it easy every once in a while. Then you would package all of these gifts in a shoe box, as tightly as you could, and bring it to the church, where it would be sent with many other shoe boxes to a remote village somewhere far, far away. To emphasize the vast farness of the village, the British woman narrating the video told us that our gifts would be taken across the sea on a barge, then flown in small planes to even smaller landing strips, then carried on camelback to the needy children who awaited their arrival. The camel on the video screen chomped on nothing, the way camels are wont to do, then turned his head and stared at us.

"You could go to a Family Dollar and pick up a bunch of presents for only a few bucks," the woman organizing the fund-raiser said. "You could get enough presents to fill four Christmas shoe boxes without spending more than you would on dinner."

I sat there trying to estimate how much it would cost to ship all of these shoe boxes via next-day barge and priority camel, how long it would take Al Gore to clean up the smog and exhaust created by the trip, and how much the children of Bolivia or Malaysia would actually even *want* anything from the Family Dollar store. I wondered why we didn't send the money-we-would-have-spent-on-dinner directly to the remote villages so they could buy those things in their own countries and bolster their own economies.

you would also throw in a toy or two, because even third-world children like to take it easy every once in a while.

Additionally, we had no idea who these packages were being sent to, so the gifts inside were no more personal than what was originally created in the factories from where the products were once shipped. You could try to show a bit of Christmas cheer by wrapping it in your best paper, or going out of your way to get the toothbrush with a cartoon character. But then, which character? You had no way of knowing if the toothbrush would end up with a boy or a girl, a teenager or a toddler.

Other people must have had similar qualms, because our church didn't sponsor that particular activity again.

• • •

On the contrary, it is lovely to see the smile start at someone's lips after they've opened the perfect present. Perfect presents, I've found, generally say "I know you"; and validation like that is hard to come by. Likewise, very un-perfect presents seem to say the opposite. My dad still tells the story of one Christmas when he received only two presents from his parents: a dish drainer and a pair of black tennis shoes. And no one was wearing black tennis shoes, not even the geeky kids.

That Christmas disappointed him so much that when he became a father many years later, he promised himself he'd never let his children experience that same disappointment. Even though our family was never rich or even economically stable (my mom says they went into debt every December), Christmases were full of enough discarded wrapping paper and recycled bows to decorate the city. Dad would take Matchbox cars that were packaged in threes out of their packages and wrap them separately so everyone had more to open. As my brother and I listened intently from our twin beds for the sound of Santa's sleigh bells on Christmas Eve, we knew that we were loved, even though we didn't know that Dad was the one shaking the sleigh bells.

Nick's mother was right, I think, in reminding Nick that Jesus' birth should be, for Christians, the center of our Christmas gift giving. But perhaps there's more to it than simply continuing a tradition that the wise kings started. I remember being taught a song for a children's choir at church when I was maybe ten or eleven years old. I have no idea how the tune went, and the lyrics (and hand motions—because you *know* there must have been hand motions) are gone from my memory, too. But for some reason, the sentiment was mind-blowing for me, and I haven't forgotten it: Jesus came into the world as a gift.

I find it kind of funny that the song had such a profound impact on me. The idea is not a novel one; it feels as if every other Christmas song on the radio is some variation on this theme. Plus, I am not the type to wallow in the overly sentimental, especially around Christmastime. I have been hassled by many friends for my dislike of "The Little Drummer Boy," for instance. I thought everyone hated the "pa-rum-pa-pa-pumming" (which occurs twenty-one times in the song! Twenty-one!) I was wrong. It turns out that song is *much* beloved by everyone but me for its beautiful, if completely falsified, story of a boy who just wanted to play his stinking drum for the baby Jesus. While I have no problem changing the radio station every time the familiar pa-ruming comes on, I might burst into tears of gratitude if I ever hear the Jesus-as-gift chorus again. I know, I know: I'm a total hypocrite. If I meet the little drummer in heaven, I will have to apologize.

My pastor, Tim, has said that some things are sentimentalized because they are very difficult to comprehend, and maybe that is the case with presents and songs about presents. Being reminded of the greatest gift, every year, is a beautiful thing to celebrate. The gift of Jesus is so personal that it cuts to the very interior of our hearts, for he knows the depth of our sorrows and inadequacies, and he loves us so much that he left the heavens—the right hand of the Father—to descend to a barn and show us how to be.

We are known.

Our call to be like Christ means that we're to *be* gifts to each other. We are to know each other, fill the needs we see, give of our selves sacrificially and generously. This is a far bigger commitment than forking over the money for a PlayStation or a shiny sweater, but if wrapping something up can be even a small indication of this beautiful ideal, I say bring on the bows.

Sam was a little boy at our church who had just turned three. For Christmas that year, many people gathered at his parents' small apartment to celebrate. He was one of the only youngsters at our fledgling church at the time, so he was spoiled with presents. When they handed him his first wrapped gift, he exclaimed, "Tractor!" The first gift was not a tractor. It was okay, though, because many more gifts still sat on the table in front of him. The next, although Sam was sure of it and couldn't stop foretelling it at the top of his lungs, was not a tractor. (It was a book of poems. Sam had not yet had much experience in the art of guessing Christmas presents. He didn't even shake it.) We opened presents for a good twenty minutes, everyone, by this time, waiting with bated breath. But still no tractor. Then the gifts were gone. It wasn't until two late-coming friends showed up and handed Sam a package that he got what he wanted. I don't know if Sam was more pleased by the tractor or all the shouts for joy that rang up at its unveiling. I know, for me, it was the latter.

> *if wrapping something up can be even a small indication of this beautiful ideal, i say bring on the bows.*

Christmas

making space

❧

Incarnation means that all ground is holy ground
because God not only made it but walked on it, ate
and slept and worked and died on it. If we are
saved anywhere, we are saved here.

—FREDERICK BUECHNER

Though you're not supposed to say it, there were students who
I, even as an idealistic, wide-eyed, first-year teacher, wished
would move out of the district, drop out of high school, or
even spontaneously combust into a pile of ash that we'd dump
into the trash along with the contents of the pencil sharpener.
Not very many, but there were a few. Like spectators at a NAS-
CAR race, these students were the ones on the edge of their
seats hoping, praying, that you would turn too sharp and send
your billion-dollar car hurtling headlong into a wall advertis-
ing Axe Fragrance Spray or Flamin' Hot Cheetos. Or at least
they wanted the overhead projector screen to fall on you. They
lived to see their teachers fail.

Juan was not one of these students. Loud, imposing,

unapologetic, a known gang member destined never to graduate, Juan was one of the screwups I liked. I *wanted* to teach this kid, rehabilitate him, inspire him by comparing ancient Shakespearean verse to modern 50 Cent songs. This, I was hoping, would somehow give him the fervor to change his life. I thought about buying a leather jacket so the similarities between me and Michelle Pfeiffer's *Dangerous Minds* character would be even more striking, but I was too broke and too meek to pull off the necessary badassery, so I scrapped that idea early on.

Despite being a known felon, Juan was one of the few students in a rather hostile English class who I felt was rooting for me. He had a dopey grin that peeked out from under a mustache that was much thicker than seemed natural on a high school junior, and he sat near the wall, leaning on it with just the right amount of weight to achieve the laid-back demeanor that assured his classmates he didn't care a lick about whatever was going on in class. But he was never rude to me, always referred to me as "Miss," and didn't seem at all angry that a nervous and eager teacher-in-training was replacing the relaxed and seasoned Mrs. Psalter, who kept the students from burning down the building with funny references to her pretend celebrity boyfriend, Johnny Depp. Her top pedagogical concern was getting through the day, and most of the students seemed on board with this idea. I, however, was not. You can't change lives and impact children by just getting through the day, I thought. And I only had a semester.

For two weeks, I did everything short of begging to entice

the students to read *Their Eyes Were Watching God:* I made up games, I read important passages aloud, I showed movie clips, I drew character charts, I instigated role-playing. Nothing worked, and I could sense the class, which was primarily made up of girls, giving me the collective evil eye. And though I was five years, a husband, and two degrees out of high school, those high school feelings of excruciating inadequacy sprang up in my chest. They didn't like me, and they took every chance they could to tell me so. When the overhead projector actually did come inches from falling on me, probably knocking me unconscious, most of the girls snickered and rolled their eyes at each other. They counted off the days until I would be out of their lives forever.

despite being a known felon, juan was one of the few students in a rather hostile english class who i felt was rooting for me.

Teaching is one of those professions you learn only by doing. No one can prepare you in advance for the many sorts of disciplinary actions you'll have to take over the course of a day, whether it is admonishing a girl for the thong under-wear sticking out of her pants or calling for backup from the administration because a student is so angry he's sent the front podium toppling over. You learn because the students test your boundaries the same way children test their parents', and because you have no choice but to *handle it, for the love of God.* You are the grown-up. The problem with student teaching, at least for me, was that I was far from being grown up. Every morning when I got dressed, I chose suits with sharp lines and high, matronly buttons. I didn't want to be stopped on my way to the staff parking lot for trying to ditch school. Not again.

The weekend after Mother's Day, I was exhausted. We were only a month until the year's end, and each day of facing that fourth-hour class was grating. I woke up with a pile of heavy nerves languishing on my stomach. I worried about the day's lesson and about teacherly authority and about the particular looks that one particular girl gave me every single day. I tried to convince myself that Scarlett O'Hara was right about tomorrow being another day, but I did not believe myself; instead I believed that tomorrow is exactly the same as all the days before it, and I, by extension, was screwed.

Walking into class in my Ann Taylor suit and heels, I smiled like a politician. I made jokes like a politician—wishing they were funny but knowing they were not, then wishing that people would at least appreciate the fact that I was trying my damndest to be hip and relatable. (In a moment of desperation, I almost made a Johnny Depp joke—but that would have made it clear I was trying too hard. Mrs. Psalter had the market on Johnny Depp jokes.) I wanted to be authoritative but approachable. Firm but funny. Strict but cool. Unfortunately, these conflicting desires only served to make students wonder if I was suffering from multiple personality disorder. I gave them an early lecture on the importance of doing their assigned readings (the quiz results assured me they were not), then tried to switch gears to remove the iciness from their stares.

in a moment of desperation, i almost made a johnny depp joke.

"How was your weekend?" I asked the group. The politician's smile was back. "Did you do something nice for your mothers?"

"I was stabbed," said Vincent, an oafish kid with a five-o'clock shadow who sat in front. *He has got to be joking,* I thought to myself. Then he lifted up his shirt to show us where.

The next ten minutes of class were devoted to hearing the story. I was at a loss for how to handle the situation, so Mrs. Psalter chimed in occasionally from her desk in the corner. The other students in class didn't have much to add; no one could top Vincent's response, after all, and they didn't want me to get the impression that they had actually listened to or cared about my question in the first place.

When I was a young girl pretending to be a teacher, I set up rows of stuffed bears and Barbie dolls who usually minded me. There were no students so out of line that I willed them to spontaneously combust. There were no students, in fact, who didn't smile appreciatively and warmly at my efforts to improve their otherwise stagnant lives. I remember checking off names on my roster, making friendly comments to each pupil, breezily adjusting my mother's scarf around my neck. Stabbings, thong underwear, swearwords, and cement frowns had no place in my classroom then, and at twenty-three I was still the sort of girl who bristled at the mention of those things. The F-word made me cringe. I called it the F-word, too, not even allowing the syllables of the real word to form in my mouth or in my mind. Truth be told, I was not world-weary enough to be in front of a classroom of real, hardened students. I wanted the bears back, but I also didn't want to fail these people. I kept trying.

"How about you, Juan? How was your weekend?" I handed him a graded work sheet and raised my eyebrows.

"Good," he answered, from under a brimmed hat. He looked up at me, right into my eyes. "I hung out with my moms," he said, pluralizing the title as a term of affection or maybe just bad number agreement.

"Yeah?" I asked.

"Yeah. Got her some flowers. Candy." Juan smiled. A handsome smile, too. Boyish and charming. For the first time, I saw in him traces of what he must have been like as a toddler, mischievous but innocent and sweet.

"That's great," I said, barely able to contain the small high I was getting from the connection we were making.

"I love her, man." He laughed and paused for reflection. "She lets me grow my pot in our backyard."

I go to church at a high school now. Every week, a crew of volunteers arranges metal stacking chairs into rows in the theater at Olathe Northwest High School. Another team is in charge of aesthetics, making the space look less like a high school and more like a church. They are called the Environment Team, and they come equipped with Chinese lanterns, drapes of colored fabric, gauzy tablecloths, candles with electric wicks, and, of course, a large wooden cross. They do a good job, the Environment Team, but the first time my husband and I visited the church, I couldn't help but think about the last time I was in a high school theater: my students at a different Northwest High were watching a video on the perils of drunk driving. It was the week before prom. The video was graphic. It hit a little too close to home because a girl at the school had died only a few months before because she was drunk and behind the wheel. The students pretended the video was lame, acted out by snickering through some of the gorier pictures and texting their friends instead of listening to the EMT who was presenting.

For a few weeks, the space at church was unnerving for me. I kept wanting to mark fellow congregants tardy when they weren't seated by the time the band began to play, or scold them for whispering during the sermon. I'm not sure why the disciplinarian in me was summoned. If teachers were only in the business of punishment, Judge Judy could probably do a fairly good job. Many nonteachers don't realize how much of the school day is spent maintaining order, or how much of a teacher's after-school thoughts are directed toward solving behavior problems. They wonder why more teaching doesn't get done, but they haven't thought about how students' abilities range so drastically, how many students don't appreciate or enjoy learning, or how some parents are forced to work so much that they aren't there to make sure a child learns respect for other people. They also don't consider that, when you get right down to it, all people are sometimes selfish jerks, whether they are seated behind a school desk, an architect's desk, or an executive's desk. It's partly the job of a teacher to

i kept wanting to mark fellow congregants tardy when they weren't seated by the time the band began to play, or scold them for whispering during the sermon.

help students understand how to behave in a group of selfish jerks, to put their own jerkiness on hold, and to be gracious to others who are also struggling to control their inner jerks. A classroom is nothing if not a thirty-person sampling of society at large, after all.

So Redemption Church reminded me, every Sunday, of how corrupt the world can be. Memories of marijuana stories and inappropriate text messaging, of how inept I used to be at keeping students from insulting and offending one another, kept invading my worship experience.

When I was young, attending church in the main sanctuary was known as "going to big church." I did most anything I could to get out of going, because even though it sounded exciting, going meant following a long list of rules. The only time I can remember actually enjoying big church was when the youth group had an overnighter in the sanctuary and my friends and I slid in sleeping bags down the stairs that led to the sound booth and army-crawled under the rows and rows of seats we'd been forced to sit still in for years. Otherwise, big church meant closing your eyes for prayer and closing your mouth for the sermon. It's a miracle that anything at all could be open in that sort of an environment.

Despite the drudgery of obeying them, the rules of big church did create a more sacred-looking space. The Christmas greens were always well fluffed and glistening with canned snow, the words to the hymns were grammatically correct, and the titles sparkled in Old English fonts. A Bible and a tiny pencil resided in each chair pocket, beckoning congregants to take copious and holy notes on the sermon. In the wood of

the altars, the reflection of bulbs from the majestic light fix-
tures shined up at you as you knelt, and you could be sure that
the janitor had vacuumed the carpet last night so the knees
of your pants wouldn't get dirty. The rules of conduct meant
that people smiled, that most women wore nylons and most
men wore ties, and that voice levels would be appropriately
modulated to respect the austerity of the high-ceilinged room.
When the youth group band was invited to lead worship one
morning a year, we scrapped the fast songs, the ones that we
liked, and made the drummer stick a pillow in the hollow of
his bass drum to dampen the sound. (Even with the modifica-
tions, I noticed an old man in the third row with his hands
over his ears.)

I wouldn't be so presumptuous to maintain that keeping a
space sacred, in whatever way possible, is always a bad thing.
I dress up for church for precisely that reason—pencil skirts
and floral dresses make me feel like I'm doing something
active to remind myself that Sunday morning is supposed to
be "set apart"—one definition of the word *holy*. Sometimes,
I am one of the only people in the service who is dressed up.
Our pastor, Tim, is usually in jeans and a baseball cap, and
it's difficult to miss the mismatched and often dirty clothing
of the homeless people who sit in the front row. But dressing
up doesn't mean much to Tim, or to my husband, who is the
associate pastor at our church. Scott says that people in hell
will probably be forced to wear a suit and tie, so obviously
breaking out the formal wear doesn't speak to Scott's worship
experience the same way it does mine. We all find our own
ways to make a place holy or sacred.

Still, I struggled with how a high school could possibly be a holy space. I'd seen too much. My feeling is probably akin to what residents of the Holy Land feel when tourists and believers make their pilgrimages to a "mecca" they have seen ravaged by years of war and violence. Or maybe how the Magi felt upon arriving at the tiny stable where the Christ child was born. (We romanticize it with our intricately carved and painted Christmas nativity scenes, but the crèche couldn't have been sweet, regal, or even sanitary.) The wise men must have wondered if their directions were a bit off, pulling up in front of a measly dirt stable and then rechecking the address they'd gotten from the star or the dream or the tea leaves, looking at each other and muttering things like "Surely not!" with high and haughty pitches in their voices. I imagine them as sounding British.

It's possible that most of us totally misunderstand what *holy* means. Writer and theologian Frederick Buechner thinks that modern believers tend to overspiritualize the whole thing—the way God speaks, the way we're to behave, the way we should approach God. "One of the blunders religious people are particularly fond of making," he writes, "is the attempt to be more spiritual than God."[1] This is just one of the reasons why Buechner, rather than Johnny Depp, is *my* pretend boyfriend. He writes about how Jesus always comes into the middle of real life, "not in a blaze of unearthly light, not in the midst of a sermon, not in the throes of some kind of religious daydream. . . . He never approached on high, but always in the midst."[2] It's true of Jesus' birth, his ministry, and his otherworldly appearances after his death on the cross. He spent his time in the unholiest of places, and, by his very presence, transformed them. The place and circumstances of his birth, then, become shockingly significant and symbolic of the way he showed love. It's not much of a stretch to believe that Jesus, if he attended church today, would probably go to a place where nylons and ties are scarce, where homeless people show up in clothing that hasn't been washed, and where teenagers slide down the stairs in sleeping bags. I don't know that for a fact; I just have a hunch.

Theologian John Milbank (he's *actually* British, by the way) argues that the whole idea of the "secular" is totally imagined, created, and put into place by human beings—perhaps beginning sometime around the Reformation or early Enlightenment. He maintains that any sort of divide or separation that can categorize some things as "sacred" and others "secular" undermines, or at least counts out, the incarnation of Christ. Because if Christ came to earth as a human being, had a mother who was among the most oppressed and disregarded of her time, and died a criminal's death on a cross, how can we

> *jesus spent his time in the unholiest of places, and, by his very presence, transformed them.*

determine what is holy and what is not? Certainly not by our own standards, which not only fluctuate with time but also are intrinsically flawed by bias and egotism. Our standards would have easily put Jesus into the unsacred category. Besides, there is hardly a way for anyone to say what or who might be outside God's glorious provision and love. It's why extremist churches who profess GOD HATES FAGS on their protest signs or television evangelists who assert that entire countries of people are destined for hell or regular, everyday churchgoers who harbor hate in their hearts against people who don't agree with them are absolutely, fundamentally wrong. There is nothing that was not created by God, no one who might be too far from His grace, not one iota of creation that was not set apart for Him. So then, Milbank says, all of it is sacred. All of it.

Five years of teaching has changed me enough that I no longer have Michelle Pfeiffer delusions (I do still dream about blush that could give me those cheekbones, though). I am not surprised by the curse words, the inattention, the glares, or the threats—for the most part, anyway. They come with the gig, and though the job is more difficult when the students are real, imperfect people, I wouldn't go back to the stuffed versions. The bears and Barbies would behave perfectly, but they have no capacity for love. They don't surprise you with funny quips or ask tough questions that make you think. And they have no real need for a teacher.

Lately, I have become more comfortable in the unique backdrop of my church, and I don't think it has to do with the gauzy cloth and electric candles. I took my shoes off during the Christmas Eve service last year. It's one of the only services of the year where children are present in big church, and, since half of our congregation is under the age of twelve, many more bodies filled the seats. Sniffles, shouts, cries, laughter—all the sounds associated with being a child—drowned out the sounds I was used to. Usually, I try not to base my faith off emotions, which are often fickle and deceiving, but sometimes—like this particular time—that is impossible. Sometimes emotions well up and overtake me. They come out in tears or shouts or laughter or deep breaths. This time, all I could think to do was take off my shoes. I was remembering Moses and the burning bush and God vocalizing to him, "Do not come near here; remove your sandals from your feet, for the place on which you are standing is holy ground." I didn't care that the carpet was filthy. I still don't.

Epiphany

how to play

GETTING STARTED

My son Miles, at one and a half, was learning how to share or, as the saying goes, "to play well with others." At first, he wasn't very good at it. He didn't quite understand that the world and all the toys in it were not made expressly for him. I remember the first time another child in the church nursery reached for a toy Miles was holding. He got visibly annoyed. His little brow line constricted like a caterpillar in motion, his hand darted to protect the threatened object, and he turned away in a self-righteous huff. He was a smaller version of Kanye West. I suppose I was partly to blame for this, because until his sister Genevieve was born, Miles never had much competition for the trucks and balls and colorful pianos that littered our living room floor; likewise, he had never really experienced the joys of playing with other children. Other children were, in fact, a rather elusive concept to Miles. I knew it wouldn't be long before he was running around with a crowd, but at that age he, along with the rest of his peers, just seemed to be eyeing each other suspiciously.

That's not to say that those same peers didn't hold influence over each other. When I first enrolled Miles in day care, I couldn't believe that the teachers expected him to sleep on a cot, inches above the ground, in the same room as the other five children in class.

"He won't do it," I told Scott. "He'll be too interested in what's going on around him. He'll get up. He'll want to play."

But his teacher was confident. "When he sees the rest of the kids going to sleep," she said, "he'll sleep, too. It happens all the time."

And sure enough, by the end of that first week, Miles knew exactly what to do. His peers had shown him the rules of the room. He also copied the way the other kids drank from their big-kid cups and how they went down the bright orange slide in the corner of the room.

Though I had tried teaching him those same skills at home, I never had the sort of quick success these toddlers had. It was as if I was the one getting a lesson in peer pressure. "Yes, it begins this early," those children were telling me. "You're just the mom. You don't understand."

My mother says that we don't grow out of it either. She works at an assisted living facility and consistently notices how easily the seniors she works with fall in line with what's popular: if one person (especially the dashing older man with the winning smile or the bubbly woman with the huge family) shows an interest in movie night, more will flock to the same activity the next week.

We were made for interaction with each other, to be in relation with one another. It's how we learn and how we grow.

GAME PLAY

First Turn

The first game I can remember playing as a kid was Monopoly. I was around six or seven. It was a version that my cousin Stephanie and I had invented, as close to the real rules as we could understand, but still, probably, a far cry from the way the Parker Brothers intended it. I was the banker; she was in charge of the real estate. Both of us did business in the backyard, on the concrete patio across from the pool. In our bathing suits, usually, we'd bend our legs in ways adults can only remember bending to sit across from each other on our carefully laid-out towels. I always chose the little dog as my token. She was the boat. These things never changed.

Every time we got together, we played. I was meticulous about putting the pieces away correctly—rubber bands around the money, all the different denominations of money grouped together, all the way up to the golden five hundreds. My little brother, only four or five, often bent and crumpled the bills, so I'd smooth them down as best I could manage. The pieces were bagged with the dice, the board folded flat. It felt grown-up to take care of the game this way. At some point, we lost one of the orange property cards—New York Avenue—and had to re-create it with markers and pens. I remember how carefully we cut out card stock in the same size and shape as the other cards, how we figured out the value of rent— with or without houses and hotels—by analyzing the cards we still had, how we colored

in our bathing suits, usually, we'd bend our legs in ways adults can only remember bending to sit across from each other.

in a thick band of orange at the top where the property name went. This makeshift card still resides with my Monopoly game, and though we don't use it in real play with the updated board, I can't bear to throw it out.

Our games were often interrupted by other activities: running through the sprinklers, being called in for lunch, riding bicycles around the cul-de-sac. Our younger siblings played sometimes, but they usually lost interest fairly early, so we'd dump their pieces back into the lid from whence they came and continue. Monopoly was serious business for Stephanie and me. Since I was older and was making up the majority of the rules, I usually won. But it made us feel sophisticated—the buying and selling of property, the careful counting out of numbered spaces and numbered bills, the orderly taking of turns.

It's difficult to say why board games, and this one in particular, appealed to me. I scoffed at sports like football and baseball because of the sheer waste of time they seemed to be. To put it as cultural anthropologist Clifford Geertz did in an essay analyzing Balinese cockfighting, these events "make nothing happen." He continues: "Men go on allegorically humiliating one another and being allegorically humiliated by one another, day after day, glorying quietly in the experience if they have triumphed, crushed only slightly more openly by it if they have not. *But no one's status really changes.*"[1] The obsession with winning games has been known to make grown men weep or paint their flabby

we taught each other good strategy, and we gave each other loans in order to extend the game.

middles with primary colors, to cause either subsequent loot-ing or parading in the streets, to encourage the use of foghorns indoors. It just can't be healthy.

Yet while the paper money in the game never translated into real money, backyard Monopoly seemed to matter, some-how. So Stephanie and I kept passing Go, losing turns, buying hotels, paying rent. We taught each other good strategy, and we gave each other loans in order to extend the game.

Subsequent Turns

The game I played most often with my high school friends was MASH. It involved inserting the names of the cutest boys you could think of into a fortune-telling-type chart that would decide your future husband. The magic chart would also decide your career, your car, the number of kids you and Mr. Cutest Boy You Could Think Of would produce, and whether you would all live happily in a Mansion, an Apart-ment, a Shack, or a House—MASH. We weren't kidding any-one, though. None of the other details mattered as long as you got the right husband. If you were feeling snarky, you would include in your list of cutest boys the names of your friends' crushes. Just to keep things interesting. One day, a few friends and I covered an entire mirrored closet door with MASH games written in dry-erase markers. The three of us had dif-ferent charts that looked almost identical. (There were only so many cute boys in the rather small California town I grew up in. Hemet was mostly a retirement community, so unless you were trolling the local nursing home, pickin's were slim.) Everyone knew who had dibs on whom, so if the MASH chart turned out unfavorably, we would scrap it and try again. Even fate can be temporarily confused, we believed, so we kept playing until the Pats and Matts and Jakes scrawled on the closet door ended up in the correctly destined girl's winning chart.

This is probably how I would view a tarot-card reading, if I ever decided to get one—just keep going back until you get a fortune you like.

MASH kept girls in check, made sure that no one wanted zero kids and a career instead, no one was going to fall for the crazy punk kid in her English class, and nobody was going to keep her dreams to herself. To some extent, I needed to feel this sense of sameness. We were entrenched in a period of life when fitting in was important. I wanted to know I wasn't weird. I wanted to know that someone else wanted the same things I did. I wanted confirmation that my lack of boyfriends didn't mean I was destined to be alone for the rest of my life. And MASH was a great equalizer, too. Even the most unpopular girl had the right to put the hot baseball player on her MASH chart. She even had the right to keep playing until her mansion was populated with his three children. These same packs of girlfriends and I would go to football games, arms linked, outfits coordinated, and steps measured like the Redcoats. We went everywhere like this: the mall, the beach, the bathroom. I have a picture of me and seven of my closest girlfriends at our eighth-grade dance; none of us had dates, but all of us had barrel-curled bangs. It is no wonder it took me years to get a boyfriend—who among thirteen-year-old men would dare infiltrate an army of helmet-haired girls? We found safety in numbers, hairspray, and anonymity. Like the silly gazelle on those *National Geographic* specials, we did our best to look the same and never roam too far away from the rest of the herd. We were testing our identities. Hardly anyone was brave enough to try an identity of her own, wander too far from the safety of the group, as she might get eaten alive by a leopard or a senior boy. This is probably one reason the early nineties hairstyles happened at all. One girl decided that big bangs should be more than a theory, and everyone else went along with it.

Quite the opposite, a game we played in youth group was hell-bent on singling out its players, and it made my gazelle-like instincts twitchy. The game was called "If You Love Me, Honey, Would You Please Just Smile." The person designated as "It" (already a bad sign for anyone dedicated to conformity) would stand in the middle of a circle of other people. The goal was to get someone to smile by saying the phrase for which the game is named. And my peers would go to great lengths to garner a smile: they'd choose the most unlikely targets, speak with saccharine in their voices, dance like fairies, sweep their fingers up and down people's arms in exaggerated flirtatiousness, fall to their knees in earnest begging. On evenings we played this game, I would cower in my hard-backed plastic chair. I was far too shy to produce the sort of antics necessary to get a smile. And if your target didn't crack a smile, you'd be forced to keep uttering those insidious words to different targets until someone finally did. I knew that if I became "It," I'd never return to being "Not It,"

we found safety in numbers, hairspray, and anonymity.

so I made it my goal to be the most stoic freshman girl there. In four years of youth group, I never once had to be "It" in "If You Love Me, Honey, Would You Please Just Smile." Even when people started realizing I was the only one who hadn't laughed, I kept my poker face. They'd purposely aim for me, the rest of the group egging them on, but sheer determination and ice-cold fear won out, and I stayed glued to my seat round after round.

VARIATION: Team Rules

The first game of Dutch Blitz my three college friends and I played happened on a road trip the four of us took across the country. It was the summer after our freshman year, and we were smack-dab in the middle of America: Ponca City, Oklahoma. Ponca City boasts nothing of note but the Marland Estate, the mansion of an oil tycoon that you can tour in a little under an hour. We had done that. And we had already spent hours in conversation through Las Vegas, Albuquerque, and wherever the Hoover Dam is, so we needed something to do besides talk to each other.

Now that we're grown women with husbands, careers, children, and advanced degrees, we still get admittedly crazy when the Dutch Blitz cards come out. This is often, considering that we've played in at least seven different states and in the bride's rooms before three of our four weddings. Melissa's voice gets louder, Angie is immediately off to find something to use as a score sheet, Lindsey reminds everyone of how Angie physically assaulted her that one time before a match in Nashville.

I get quiet before these matches, and although I am often the one to suggest a game, I am also usually the one who ends up in last place. Dead last. The kind of last where any sane person would swear off the game in order to avoid future embarrassment.

Our husbands find it difficult to be in the same room with us when a Dutch Blitz game is going on. They become unwillingly privy, yet again, to sides of their wives that normally remain hidden under layers of manners and years of pretending to be grown-up. The game itself is fast-paced, or as the packaging describes, a "vonderful goot game" in which each player tries frantically to get rid of her pile of cards. In getting rid of cards, there is no rule against calling other players derogatory names, flinging entire bodies across the table in the pursuit of the goal, or "accidentally" knocking/shoving/pushing somebody else's hand away from her goal. There is a rule, however, regarding when to start. Everyone has to be ready, and the dealer must say "Go" before any card flipping can begin. We play messy, but we also play fair.

We have that first game on videotape. In the footage, Melissa tries to explain the rules—she's detailed in the way she describes exactly how one should flip her cards, how she should remove a pile of ten when she "finishes" it, how she is to announce a win if one were to occur. It's like she's describing brain surgery. (Since that first game, we've also learned that Melissa often breaks the same rules she so clearly articulated that Oklahoma evening around her dining room table. When I said we play fair, I meant only when we can't get away with playing dirty.) Angie,

Lindsey, and I look nervous. We all stand around the table, our cards in our hands, our eyes darting this way and that in an effort to be quick, even though we don't know the rules well enough to have developed a strategy. Melissa's mom laughs jovially and loudly somewhere in the background.

We planned the road trip after casual discussion of it one night in Melissa's and my San Diego college dorm room. "That would be fun," we'd all said. I never really thought it would happen. It's like how swimming with dolphins or renting a rocket ship to the moon would be fun. I didn't know Angie very well at the time, though, didn't realize she'd already begun mentally planning the cheapest (or, more accurately, the freest) places to stay along the map: in Las Vegas on the floor of her boyfriend's brother's apartment, in Memphis with someone's former youth pastor and his wife, in Oklahoma with Melissa's parents. We'd end up, finally, in Florida at Angie's parents' condo on the beach. The projected budget and itinerary were finished and ready to be finalized before finals week began. She was the type of person who knew she'd be an accountant even as a freshman student and had already begun hoarding briefcases for her future career, tablecloths for her future dining room, and baby clothes she found on clearance racks for her future child. (Some of the clothes are blue, some pink. When she can't accurately control something, she just prepares for all possible scenarios.)

when i said we play fair, i meant only when we can't get away with playing dirty.

We were friends that first year of college, but we weren't good friends yet. In fact, I had few good friends at college that year. Most of my friends were still at home, an hour's drive away, as I was holding on to high school friends who I felt would be the ones I'd grow old with and have forever. I resisted making new friends and new memories because I liked my old friends and old memories. I've always resisted moving on, and it is one of my life's regrets that I am slow to find pleasure in newness, but I'm working on it. Back then I was just stubborn, so it took the better part of a year before I decided to pour any emotional energy at all into new relationships. The road trip shook the resistance right out of me.

When I look back on it now, it's easy to see the trip as symbolic: we were four girls finishing our freshman year at college, on the verge of finding out who we were becoming. It was an emotional journey as well as a physical one—a classic story of maturation. So much would change the following year: Melissa would change her major—trading in her bassoon for a microscope—Angie would move back to her hometown of Nashville, I would meet Scott, Lindsey would join a traveling singing group. But memory and hindsight tend to give you the perspective of a rearview mirror: objects may be more obvious than they first appear. Back then, we just couldn't believe our parents had let us go. It wasn't symbolic of anything. It was adventure and action.

HOW TO WIN

As we traveled east, Lindsey (who is a Northern California native) acquired something of an accent. The more Midwesterners we spent time with, the more Midwestern Lindsey would begin to sound. The more Southerners we spent time with, the more Southern Lindsey would sound. It was as if the language was simply melting in her mouth, like a winter snow that is not quite cold enough, that rests too heavily in bushes and grasses, sinking into cracks and crevices, conforming to their shapes. We used to tease Lindsey about this slow morphing of her dialect. "Where are you from?" we'd ask with rolled eyes. "I don't know!" Lindsey would say in Las Vegas; "Ah don't know!" she'd drawl in Nashville. But her chameleon's accent was only an obvious manifestation of what was happening on a deeper level in our lives: a slow entwining of experiences, quirks, passions, irritants. A morphing that didn't replace the person I was with someone new, but gently shaped her into a better version of me. This was a slow process, one that did not force change or discard eccentricities or nuances of personality like the MASH games might have, one that made us more alike in some ways, more aware of our differences in others. Little displays of the qualities we admired in each other would pop up throughout the day, and by that time, I was learning how to pay attention to them.

Writer Robert Benson says that "reaching out" is giving someone else a sense of who God is.[2] If this is true, then reaching out in its truest sense must happen most often among those who spend significant periods of time together. It must happen most often among friends, families, church families. Benson spoke about reaching out in terms of finding a calling, and how a somewhat random group of people led him to his calling—people in different states and of different vocations. Some were his closest friends, some merely popped into his life in the most mundane and superficial of ways. But each contributed, usually in ways unbeknownst to them, to Benson's construction of himself.[3] But perhaps *construction* is the wrong word. Are these people adding to our truest selves? Each one placing a new nail in the structure? Or are they helping to carve out, as Michelangelo professed to, the real self hiding in the lump of stone? Either way, work is being done. Art, in fact.

In his book *I and Thou,* Martin Buber maintains that a person "becomes an I through a You."[4] We are only ourselves in relationship to those around us. Perhaps this is why there is so much emphasis on church in the Christian heritage. Indeed, as Eugene Peterson writes, "Everything that God is and everything that we are intersects locally in the company of family and friends and the immediate circumstances of our lives. . . . God is not abstract, remote, inaccessible. Church—ordinary, local, immediate, personal—welcomes us into the company of Jesus, who is God with us, who embraces the human condition and speaks our language."[5] While many people envision church as somewhere to go on Sunday morning, somewhere to sing hymns, old or new, somewhere to give money, somewhere to get married, get baptized, or get eulogized, I don't think that is the way Jesus understood it. Or the God of the Old Testament (isn't that a funny phrase? As if God was somehow different then from now?), who discouraged his people from confining him to particular places, domesticating God's presence in the temple or even the Ark of

this morphing didn't replace the person i was with someone new, but gently shaped her into a better version of me.

the Covenant. The church is his people, living life alongside one another, giving the best of themselves to each other and to God as often as they can.

Because of ideas he's taken largely from Eastern Orthodoxy, religion professor Steve McCormick has called the church God's "new epiphany." *Epiphany,* now most often associated with a quick whiplash of understanding, means "showing" or "appearing." In the season so named, liturgical texts chronicle the life of Jesus: the journey of the Magi to his cradle, the day of his baptism when God's spirit descended upon him like a dove, his first miracle in Cana when he turned the water into wine. To me, these events seem to highlight people's abrupt discovery that Jesus was no ordinary man. He was God in skin, right in front of all those people, showing and appearing all over the place. Not in the vulgar way, of course, but still in rather uncouth and rudimentary ways. Ways unbecoming of deity, in the minds of those who were supposed to know. And then he was gone.

he was god in skin, right in front of all those people, showing and appearing all over the place.

To be God's new epiphany, then, is something of a big deal. The church is meant to be, as Christ was, a physical manifestation of God. "Ha. We are so screwed!" the sarcastic voice inside my head wants to tell you. But God wouldn't have commissioned it if He didn't think we could do it.

NOTES ON PLAY

I spoke to Melissa on the phone a little while ago. It was the first time we'd talked in about a year or so, and calls are so rare that she usually greets me with the statement "You're pregnant." (This time, I wasn't, but last time I was. So her record isn't bad.) Her journey from San Diego had taken her to Detroit; mine had taken me to Kansas City. She was leaving again, though, this time for Orlando. In the space of the two decades since we'd left our dorm room in San Diego, both Melissa and I had uprooted ourselves twice. Each uprooting meant a different city; sometimes it meant a different state.

"It's hard every time," she said. "Leaving friends. But this time it seems especially hard."

"I know," I said. "But you'll find new friends." Even as I said it, I wished I hadn't. I was trying to be encouraging, but I knew that wasn't what she wanted or needed to hear.

"Oh, I know, but these friends just seem special. Like the lifelong sort." I got jealous of Melissa's Detroit friends for a moment. I wanted her to miss me that way, even as I knew she missed me in a different way. I thought about our last day of college, sobbing as each friend packed her boxes into the back of her parents' vehicle. People told me then that I'd "find new friends," and they were certainly right. What has thoroughly surprised me was not that I found new friends, but that I discovered how thoroughly my old friends were never lost. During a time when migration happens more regularly than not—the average American moves somewhere around twelve times over the course of a lifetime—I've got friends all across the nation. Some, I may never see again. Others, I will travel many miles to visit as often as I can. Online social networking helps, keeping me abreast of what's going on in the daily lives of these geographically scattered people. But I suspect that it is not the knowledge I have of them that keeps these friends relevant and real in my life. Instead, it is the memories and recollections of otherwise inconsequential moments—losing a turn, paying the banker, rolling again—the movements of life that I was lucky enough to share with people who had chosen to spend time with me, and I with them.

Just as Geertz found of his Balinese cockfight, so Peterson intones that worship isn't "intended to make anything happen." Instead, he maintains that "worship brings us into a presence in which God makes something happen."[6] And if we are perceptive enough to count even the seemingly innocuous activities as opportunities for worship, we may, in fact, be lucky enough to see God act and work through His people. It is how we grow up, as Paul writes it in Ephesians, "healthy in God and robust in love."

Lent

the second week

I am the sort of person who could have been employed in biblical times as a weeper and mourner. I could have been paid to show up at funerals—any funeral—and cry. This I have excelled at for as long as I can remember. I cry at funerals of my loved ones, of the loved ones of loved ones, and even funerals I see on television—the funerals of loved ones who are both real and fictional. That's why I think I could kick ass at being Katie Savage, Weeper and Mourner Extraordinaire: because when I cry at funerals, it is not usually that I am crying for the deceased. For all it matters to me, the deceased could have been a jerk or a complete stranger. I believe that person ends up wherever he or she has spent his or her life getting to, that God, in His infinite wisdom, fairness, and love, has gotten that person there. (This is a vague and undefined belief, which is why I am glad that I am not responsible for deciding anything about heaven and hell. If I were in charge, I would spend all my time vacillating among sending no one to hell; sending only murderers, rapists, and bad tippers to hell; and sending anyone who refuses to use their turn signal to hell. I would be an emotionally unstable drama queen of a decision maker—an Elizabeth Taylor of deities.) To me, there is very little use in crying over or praying for a dead body; instead, I cry for those who will spend the rest of their lives missing that person, those whose lives will suddenly possess a void so deep that, no matter how many shovels you use to fill it, you will never hear the dirt hit the bottom.

My husband's grandpa Sam died during our first year of marriage. I didn't know him well, had only met him once, in fact, but I might have been the person most visibly upset at his funeral. This was rather embarrassing. Sam's wife of over forty years was sad, of course, but she was barely crying. Sam's children, my father-in-law included, were grim but also composed.

But here I was in the back row, the newest member of the family, the one who was still getting to know the names of extended relatives, the young wife of one of Sam's grandsons, doing the ugly cry. The ugly cry, as my sister-in-law Ali and I define it, is the result of crying very hard while working very hard not to. One's face becomes distorted, almost like it would look to be constipated on a roller coaster; the noises might be similar, too. The real kicker is that the harder one tries to avoid the ugly cry, the uglier it becomes. Maybe these new relatives of mine were already used to my ugly cries, as I first demonstrated my penchant for an inappropriate number of tears in front of all of them at my wedding. (The ugly cry is exponentially worse when you have a face full of makeup and a very white dress, by the way. I know this because my wedding photographer must have thought it a very sweet moment—I have dozens of pictures of this part of the ceremony that are still in the black boxes the proofs came in.) Either way, I wept and I mourned. Loudly. I thought about Sam's wife, how she would go home to an empty house, or worse, an empty reclining chair that would look so unfamiliar without the someone who had been sitting in it for so many years.

When I was sixteen, I could not cry at my friend Paula's funeral. Instead, I was at summer camp, weeping, mourning, and gnashing a few teeth around a fire pit. Death doesn't seem to care whether or not you had things planned, and I'd had summer camp planned all year, so going to Hume Lake was both a familiar experience and an extremely strange one that year. I suspect now that being at that fire pit was more healing for me than being at her funeral, because Paula had probably been sitting around that very same fire pit only a week earlier, when her church had attended camp. Something about it seemed sacred and right, like I was with her even though she was gone, like I could enjoy this one final experience with her.

I was a summer-camp kid. From the time I was in middle school, the second week of July meant that my friends and I would make the eight-hour bus trip up the mountain to Hume Lake. There were pine trees there, a lake, lots of dirt paths and big rocks, and more birds and lizards and crickets than you could shake a stick at. (One year, there were even sightings of a bear, but they called Animal Control before he could get close.) I have never been much of a nature freak, as I'm sure I made clear by my vague descriptions of the flora and fauna, but Hume Lake was a nice

the harder one tries to avoid the ugly cry, the uglier it becomes.

way to enjoy nature without having to be too far away from civilization, curling irons, and people who can tranquilize bears if need be. You could take a rowboat out on the water, but you didn't have to haul it behind your car for miles or build one out of driftwood that was dispersed across the beach; you just rented it from the tanned lifeguard by the docks. He was kind of cute, anyway, and if renting a rowboat was all it took to get him to smile at you, then I was game.

The day Paula died, only three days before we were to board the bus to Hume Lake, I was sleeping over at Anne-Marie's house. When her mother knocked softly on the door, we thought, like on most lazy summer afternoons, it was to rouse us from our sleeping in. But something had happened to Paula at camp, AnneMarie's mother told us.

Paula's church always went to Hume Lake the week before my church did; we'd hear stories of their explorations of waterfalls, the gossip of who had kissed whom, the critiques of the music in chapel. But that day, at that moment, even while the rest of her church friends were exploring and kissing and critiquing, Paula was brain-dead but alive, hooked up to machines that I, being young and full of optimism, thought somehow might save her still. It was a brain aneurysm, and it happened suddenly, in the middle of the night: after she had memorized her Bible verses for the day; after she'd complained about the food in the dining hall; after a day in the sun, paddling a canoe across water that, with the exuberant activity of teenagers with a year's worth of pent-up energy, couldn't be still. She woke up in her bunk bed with a headache. By the time they rushed her down the mountain to the hospital, she was gone. It was fast like that—like a car crash, but in the middle of the woods, and in a place that I used to think went untouched by sadness.

For me, Hume Lake had the quality that many summer camps seem to possess: the ability to stay frozen in time. It was like Grandma and Grandpa's playroom, where I knew exactly the place in the closet to find the funny-looking Barbie dolls from the 1970s and the knitted hats for dress-up, and everything held the peculiar smell of antiquity and novelty. Our charter bus would lumber up the same mountain road, stop in front of the great wooden chapel, and my friends and I would jump out. Everything would be like it was the last year, except for our suitcases, which seemed to grow with time like the hole in the ozone layer. (Now that I think about it, the same products were probably to blame for the growth of both.) We'd excitedly hike the mountain to the same cabins. Mine was called Poplar, and by chance of fate or intervention of God, it was the same cabin my mother had bunked in when she was a teenager. She said that it was the same even then. Maybe they replaced the mattresses, but that is not a fact of which I am certain, because the mattresses squeaked the same after every afternoon spent in the sun, when you're gingerly trying to find a sleeping position that won't irritate your new sunburn. The pool glistened the same, the chapel smelled the same, the milk shakes at the Snack Shack tasted the same, but most of all, the way I felt—that mix of youthful zest, spiritual expectation, and hormonal vigor—was exactly the same.

When word got out in our youth group of Paula's death, we weren't sure what to do. Did we still go to camp? Could we still have fun? Those things seemed wrong. We thought we should never have fun again, out of respect for her family or something. Moreover, we didn't *feel* like having fun. Paula was the kind of girl that everyone liked, and not because she was especially pretty or rich or gifted with giant breasts. She was just genuinely kind. This is rare in a teenaged person, and, as teenaged people ourselves, we knew it. Though she was in the in-crowd, Paula knew the names of the kids in all the different out-crowds. She waved to the kids in the "special" classes, and not out of pressure to make them feel included, but because she liked them. Though she was a senior, she talked to sophomores like me, smiled at me in the hallway. She greeted teachers and custodians, and they liked her, even though she wasn't particularly smart or involved in the cleanliness of the campus. Because of all this, Paula was nominated for Homecoming Queen, and she won by a landslide. I know because I helped count the ballots.

So this person, this near-perfect person, dies, and all the people she befriended and waved to and smiled at for the four most socially vulnerable years of life were supposed to just go to camp? Time shuffled miserably along for the hours and days following her death, but the calendar (as calendars do) moved forward at a swagger, and soon it was time to begin packing for the trip to Hume Lake. I couldn't postpone camp, and I couldn't stay home; my parents had put up too much money, I had invested too many hours in fund-raising car washes and monotonous day counting. So, I did what I did every year and remembered to pack my toothbrush.

• • •

The feeling of normalcy I had when I got off the bus was loathsome. The wind in the pine trees and the swishing of lake water against the dock whispered to me that nothing had changed, but the weight in my stomach was not from the fast food we'd stopped for along the way. *Paula is dead,* I wanted to shout back. *I refuse to enjoy this!* The camp staff was also in a state of shock. Since Hume Lake was so big, they didn't know Paula personally, but she was one of their own, and they felt the loss. The guy who led the team competitions, for example, who was one of those constantly "high on life" people who is addressed only by his initials and always seems to greet you with a handshake that involves finger-wiggling, was more subdued. He mentioned her in a bullhorn prayer once, and I understood that he shared a piece of my sorrow.

we thought we should never have fun again, out of respect for her family or something.

Little nuances of difference kept appearing, reminding me that things had changed and showing me how. Perhaps they were so small that I would have missed them at home, in the strangeness of a funeral and newspaper clippings and a paused routine. But the peculiar sameness of summer camp left me free to absorb the difference that the new year brought. "Every year is not the same as the last; each season is reminiscent but not the same as its precedent of the past year," writes Jay C. Rochelle in his article "Beginnings and Ends."[1] Though camp had not changed, I had. My experiences, my growing up, my losses, my epiphanies, my detriments, my newness, the seasons of life—when held up to ritual and pattern were obvious. I could measure them like you can a child's growth against marks on a doorframe.

I was twenty-four years old before I truly got to experience the richness of changing seasons. I grew up in Southern California, where there are really only two seasons: summer and pretty-much-summer. When my husband and I moved across the country into our first apartment in Kansas City in November, the wind bit our fingers as we struggled to pivot our monstrous brown couch up curved, concrete steps. By the end of the afternoon, our vulnerable skin and spirits were chapped. We were forced by the weather to reorder our lives. We bought gloves. Thick ones.

It is taking me a while to appreciate seasons. I love summer and pretty-much-summer and don't like unearthing my car from underneath layers of snow. I am late when there is no snow, so adding snow to the hurriedness of finding-keys-eating-breakfast-changing-the-baby-trying-not-to-look-like-the-Whore-of-Babylon-with-that-new-lipstick-color takes me from being five minutes late to being the irritating person who everyone is always waiting for. Always. Always. But this is only the beginning of the complications that a change in weather brings.

I like when getting dressed means 1 T-shirt + 1 pair of jeans + flip-flop sandals. California has conditioned me that way. I can tell you the best pair of flip-flops to buy, which ones will go with everything, which ones will not hurt the in-between of your toes—even on the first wearing. That equation is easy and doable and does not amount to a billion loads of laundry and laying-flat-to-dry. Cold weather, on the other hand, means a T-shirt layered and buried under inches of itchy wool sweaters and waterproof jackets and knitted gloves and some sort of crazy microfiber fleece head covering. (The importance of a hat I have only recently understood, after four Kansas winters—wow, those things work! I highly recommend the hat idea.) And the shoes still baffle me. I have been sliding down sidewalks in tiny heels, frozen-footed in paper-thin Converse sneakers, and soggy in sheepskin boots that are very cozy indoors but not made for slush.

I have a friend who is always advocating for a simplified life. Don't buy tons of stuff you don't need, she says. One pair of boots has lasted her since high school. For me, I can't imagine having fewer than six pairs. (Who can live so simply that they settle for black boots with an outfit that begs for brown?).

i grew up in southern california, where there are really only two seasons: summer and pretty-much-summer.

I have begun to realize it is not always good to be warm. When I consider that first winter, I remember many gloomy days of staying indoors, but more often I remember the first snow and how our tiny Maltese, Isabelle, burrowed joyfully through white flakiness piled higher than she was tall. It was her first experience with snow, too. Then, I remember a few months later bending over one of the planter boxes in our front yard, amazed at the spark of green that was beginning, like an ember, to light up the desolate, dead-looking dirt. I suppose I'd learned after only one winter that new life looks much better after a cold, hard, long bout with death and freeze. So now we celebrate the last few warm nights of the autumn with the rest of Kansas Citians by wearing tank tops and strolling Loose Park with our dogs. Outdoor shopping malls and restaurant patios are full, everyone happy for one final drag on fall's sweetness before the sobering onset of winter. On those nights, even when the shivers creep in, we refuse to put on jackets because of the sheer principle of the matter.

There are not nights like these in San Diego. Most nights are warm, so people don't appreciate, at least not all at the same time, how comfortable and comforting the weather can be. They aren't forced to recognize the change in seasons, so they simply don't.

Seasonlessness is attractive, and our culture is drawn to it. I am drawn to it. We haul bananas up from Chile or Brazil or Bananaville Island, pick them up at the grocery store for ninety-nine cents a pound, and don't realize the fact that bananas are miraculous when the temperature is below zero. Likewise, I see many young women, and even men, around Kansas City sporting tans in the middle of winter from places with names like Electric Sun, Grabba Tan, and Endless Glow.

new life looks much better after a cold, hard, long bout with death and freeze.

We are more comfortable, perhaps, than we should be, more beautiful.

Wendell Berry identifies this desire for seasonlessness as our "war against nature." In his essay "Agriculture from the Roots Up," he writes: "This [war] we have thought of as our 'enlightenment' and as 'progress.' But . . . this war, like most wars, has turned out to be a trickier business than we expected. We must now face two shocking surprises. The first surprise is that if we say and believe that we are at war with nature, then we are in the fullest sense at war: that is, we are both opposing and being opposed, and the costs to both sides are extremely high. The second surprise is that we are not winning. On the evidence now available, we have to conclude that we are losing—and, moreover, that there was never a chance that we could win."[2] He goes on to describe the ways in which agriculture has struggled from continuous overplanting, pesticides that make crops bigger and more bountiful, and the destruction we've caused by our search for the cheapest and most abundant fuels. These unnatural measures we go through to make sure we're always comfortable have their costs.

But it isn't just the earth that has suffered. In the deepest parts of our souls, I think, we long for seasons. They order our lives and our days, help us mark the passage of time, and give us something to focus upon; they return again and again, like the ocean tides and the phases of the moon. They are schedules on a larger scale, as Annie Dillard writes, "a net for catching days."[3]

My life, when I was a girl, was in no way cyclical. I didn't have the weather to help me realize change, and I was Protestant, so I didn't celebrate or even know about liturgical seasons or the church calendar. My goal was to move my faith constantly, consistently (unsustainably, I know now) upward. I hammered and clawed for the highs, planted flags in the good feelings I experienced and the number of times a hymn brought me to tears. And summer camp was another peak—steeper than the other climbs, but still uphill and upbeat. I went, I saw God in the majesty of a clear night sky, and I came down the mountain feeling like Moses after his encounters with God at Sinai. There were days, too, when I was so frustrated with the rest of the world that I could have thrown a few stone tablets of my own. Crushed them to smithereens.

The summer that Paula died was something new for me. I felt loss so fully, and no number of handsome lifeguards could help. The only thing to do in a situation like that is to embrace the drop in altitude—even at the height of my Evangelical-Feel-Good-Americanism, I couldn't utter the desultory phrases that are too often thrown about in churches after something catastrophic or sad has happened: "God wanted to get your attention," or "This is part of His plan." While I understood, even then, why people utter them, I simply didn't believe those things. I was sad. And I believed God was sad, too.

I don't know why it was so hard for me to admit that the Bible and the Byrds were right: "To every thing there is a season, and a time to every purpose under the heaven." Perhaps it has to do with wanting only half of the things that Solomon lists in that depressing little passage. I'll take the birthing but not the dying, the healing but not the killing, the dancing but not the mourning.

I returned to camp the next summer as a staff member at the Snack Shack. I supervised daily over the important task of churning milk and ice cream in a chilled metal cup. We were always busy after chapel, when the line of campers went fifteen, maybe twenty-five people deep, and most of them ordered milk shakes. One of my favorite parts of a sometimes monotonous job was watching the disparate ingredients—the crunchy Oreo cookies, the gooey hot fudge, the tangy strawberries, the chunky ice cream—spin together to form something new and wonderful.

The mixer would struggle at first. The frozen stuff would resist breaking down, the shiny hand of metal would jump a bit, the motor would moan. Then, suddenly, something would give, and the colors and textures melded together; the motor and the hand could stop struggling and do their respective jobs with more ease and grace.

Paula's family had scattered her ashes over the lake some months after her death. The summer I worked there, I often wondered where they'd ended up. I wondered if I had ever breathed a few of them in during an afternoon hike, and later I would think of what Anne Lamott wrote about ashes, about their contradictory nature: "so heavy and so light . . . impossible to let go of entirely."[4] There were nights when I looked up at the stars and remembered Paula, grew sad, grew impatient for the "kingdom come" stuff that Jesus always talked about when things would be fair and right. Bad things would happen to bad tippers, good things would happen to good tippers, nearly perfect people would live to nearly perfect ages and then die peacefully in their sleep.

But for now, we muddle through different seasons of life, trying to embrace how our motors must moan and struggle in order that we might become something better. For now: milk shakes.

getting it out

"This is going to sound kind of strange," he said.

It was late November in Kansas City. The air was crisp and chilly, and the patio of the restaurant where I was waiting tables was still almost full of guests. I was busy, but the man who had begun this already uncomfortable conversation was a customer who'd been seated in my section a few hours earlier—I figured he'd forgotten a jacket or a cell phone, or maybe he was just desperate for a date.

"Okay . . ." I said.

"Do you have about five minutes?" he asked. "We could go down by the bathroom."

I pictured the ladies' room, which is down a flight of stairs and near nothing but the huge walk-in freezer. I'd heard about stuff like this on *20/20*. What was it Barbara Walters always said to do?

"Let me explain," he said quickly, sensing my panic. The pause after his statement was long.

"You have a whisker on your chin. My friends and I noticed it earlier. It was—" He stopped. "It was glistening in the sunlight."

My mouth and neck muscles tightened as the image of a glistening whisker danced around in my head. At least this subject wasn't worthy of *20/20* coverage, but I still wasn't entirely comfortable with the conversation. I grasped at the air beneath my naked chin, scanning the patio to see how many of my current customers had overheard him. Or maybe how many of them were nodding in agreement, happy that someone finally had the guts to call attention to it.

This rogue "whisker," as he called it, had made its first appearance a few years back. While I was washing dishes in our apartment one day, my roommate Lindsey stopped me mid-dish to brush some hair away from my face. When the whisker didn't budge, she screamed, "It's attached!" and then proceeded to pull out the—as I prefer calling it—Silky Chin Hair. The skin on my chin had puckered with the effort.

I have other issues with inappropriate hair growth. My bikini line, for instance, seems continually to aspire to become a Bermuda-shorts line. (It is truly a lesson in perseverance.) But I take care of such growth so nobody else has to know it's there. With the Silky Chin Hair, the opposite occurs: while quite obvious to others, it is mysteriously elusive to me. I'd just as soon pretend that it doesn't exist, but this tactic is decidedly ineffective. When Lindsey pulled it out, the Hair was about two inches in length. *Two inches!* Another close friend, Ivy, traveled for a month with me in London, had noticed the whisker while we were floating down the Thames one afternoon, and had said nothing. Therefore, when Lindsey told her the story of my almost-beard, she wasn't surprised. Apparently, she must have thought I was purposely growing it, cultivating it for show or for entry into the record books.

But back to the man at the restaurant.

"I will give you forty dollars if you let me pluck it," he said. And though you may think I am making this up for dramatic effect, he did, in fact, use the word *pluck*. Believe me. I remember. Perfectly.

As I stood there listening to his odd request, I racked my brain for a way to get out with even a small measure of grace. Breaking into tears of embarrassment was out. That would ruin my mascara. Slapping the man swiftly on the cheek would have been satisfying (and would have bordered on Badass, which is a land into which I have only tiptoed) but still seemed a bit melodramatic. That left either walking away in a huff or, of course, letting him do his plucking.

I was already thoroughly embarrassed, even though the man assured me that wasn't his intention. (To which I sing "liar, liar, pants on fire.") There was no hiding the Silky Chin Hair at this point. The man and his friends had been discussing and contemplating it for the past four hours, it seemed, and the customers at tables sitting near us were now well aware of its existence. I couldn't pretend he was mistaken, especially when it had been *glistening* for so damn long. In fact, the man was still sort of staring at my chin now.

In American culture, there seems to be something inherently wrong with body hair. Women—and men, for that matter—

fork over millions of dollars a year to get leg, back, ear, bikini, underarm, upper-lip (and, yes, chin) hair waxed, plucked, bleached, even burned away. Funny, but there is no socially acceptable place for body hair except one, and it happens to be the most obvious and visible place on the entire body: our heads. (Men get away with it on their faces, too, but really only *some* men, and only for a while.) In the case of our head hair, we write about it in beauty magazines and talk about it on *Oprah* and include it on our secret internal lists of "What I Look for in a Mate." As for the rest of our hair, most of us choose to eradicate it.

Perhaps our aversion to body hair was inherited from ancient Egypt or Greece, where a smooth, hairless body was symbolic of beauty and youth. Or maybe it stems from a more spiritual root. In Islam, for instance, two of ten actions intended to restore the body to its original, sinless form, the *fitrah,* involve getting rid of body hair. Hair is, in this sense, a mark of corruption, a sign that we have outgrown the innocence of youth. In the Bible, too, one of the more unsavory characters in the book of Genesis, Esau, is characterized by and named for his overt hairiness, and priests would shave their heads in lament and repentance for the sin of their people. More recently, Kurt Vonnegut wrote that "the difference between pornography and art is bodily hair," and many early-Churchers must have agreed with him—they commissioned artists to paint loincloths and fig leaves over the unmentionables depicted in a variety of sacred paintings and sculptures. (The most famous of these cases involved Daniele Ricciarelli, who painted so many loincloths over so many private parts in Michelangelo's *Last Judgment* that he was nicknamed "the breeches maker.") So the association between unrighteousness and, well, hair follicles isn't a new one.

But we all have it. All of us. Why, then, was I so embarrassed by this customer's question? It was just a whisker, after all.

The answer came to me one day at the dog park. I had taken our Lab mix, Rowdy, there on the first official day of spring so he could run off some of the winter energy he'd been harboring. Rowdy had been to the dog park before, but not since the last warm day of the fall, and I suppose he'd forgotten that he actually *liked* other dogs. When I let him off the leash, he proceeded either to snap at or to mount any canine he came in contact with. He was a hurricane of inappropriate behavior, a sort of Charlie Sheen of the dog world. Other dog owners, who had obviously paid for obedience school and doggie day care, scowled at me.

I put on my most apologetic face and hurried after Rowdy to prevent him from violating a little terrier. It was to no avail. When my friend Vicki showed up a half hour later with her better-behaved dogs, I was exasperated and ready to leave.

"Why does it bother you so much?" Vicki asked. She was just the sort of levelheaded person to ask such a question.

"Because he's embarrassing the family," I responded.

"But he's a *dog*."

And she was right. He was a dog, and this behavior was natural for him. It was in his blood. I was so terribly concerned with impressing the owner of the sleek greyhounds, fitting in with the dog-park regulars, making sure that I wasn't looked at as the person most likely to have Animal Control called on her, that I had made myself nearly crazy with anxiety. This was the kind of manic concern with image that I have perfected over the years. In high school, I made sure that my dad never dropped me off at school in the primed, not-yet-painted El Camino. I am acutely aware all day if I forget to put on mascara in the morning. I obsess about issues like what the color of my living room walls or the contents of my refrigerator say about me. This needed to stop, and I knew it.

Ten minutes later, I left the dog park anyway.

It is no wonder that the unrighteousness I tend toward is the kind that is easily hidden: pride, jealousy, judgeyness. The sins of the heart, they are called. I find myself confessing those more than anything else—confessing them to God, that is. Confessing to people is more difficult. Whenever I find myself jealous of the Catholics for their worship services, so richly embedded in symbolism and ritual, I am reminded of the confession booth. Then I am quite happy to be Protestant, thank you very much.

This contradiction itself is problematic. I wonder sometimes if I don't quite believe in God as much as I claim to. Why else would I find it so easy to speak to the Divine Creator of the Universe about my petty selfishness, but not to my husband or my pastor or even a stranger? Is it because I wouldn't want *them* to think less of me?

Some of this angst regarding confession probably comes from my teenage years, as most angst seems to. Back then, my parents had a difficult marriage. There was almost no talking at all—they lived, literally, in two different sections of the house with a locked door between them. Dad came out of the back bedroom only to make himself a can of something for dinner, or if he heard the car start up and drive away. If words were spoken, they were mostly yelled above the sound of breaking dishes. The situation had made me bitter. I hated being in the same room with my parents, so I began spending dinners and nights over at my best friend Cana's house, avoiding the mess and refusing to show mercy to anyone involved in it.

I suggested more than once that we see a family therapist or even a school counselor, but Dad would always grumble something about not "airing the dirty laundry," and the subject was dropped. Not even Cana knew what was going on at my home; she wasn't allowed to know. No one but God was privy to the details of the tangled-upness of our situation until I broke into tears in the school bathroom one day, mascara running in darkened rivulets down my cheeks and into my mouth. I told her everything, and it was after that that the healing began.

> *i wonder sometimes if i don't quite believe in god as much as i claim to.*

Sin is as much a part of being human as body hair is—that much seems to be true. Even people who seem virtually sinless are at least a part of someone else's sin: they buy coffee or halter tops that were made possible by working conditions that oppress the poor, or maybe they pay taxes to support the greed and overindulgence of a wasteful and violent government. Whatever the case, we humans constantly hurt and are hurt by each other. And it is in this broken state that we all exist, each of us striving to look as put-together as possible without showing the cracks or glue.

There are at least two church seasons that beckon us to reflect on sin and repentance: Lent and Advent. Though many people don't realize it, Advent was known in the early Church as "little Lent," and that is one reason why the traditional church colors for Advent—deep purples and blues—are similar to those of the Lenten season, and why many people still fast during the time leading up to Christmas. One of the first steps in preparing for the coming of Christ is to purify the heart. It makes sense, like cleaning up before company arrives—but not like stuffing all of your junk in the hall closet and hoping that nobody opens that door. These seasons direct us toward an acknowledgment that we are all broken, every last one of us. We are a people fallen from grace, and, as Rilke writes, "all we have stammered ever since are fragments of [God's] ancient name."[1] Why ignore it any longer?

I am reminded of the woman in the Bible whose only descriptive adjective (before Jesus gets to her, anyway) is "sinful." She is the one who bows low before his feet, weeping in sorrow and repentance, and washes his feet with her tears. She uncovers her long hair (back then, and in some places still today, even exposed head hair was socially unacceptable for women) and uses it to wipe away the Jerusalem dust from in between his toes. She doesn't seem to care that her shame is out on display before all of the sinless-looking men of the city. The prophet's feet needed cleaning.

It is she, a mess of snot and tangled hair, whom Jesus blesses and forgives.

If you're wondering, I decided to let the man at the restaurant pluck the Silky Chin Hair. In one swift motion, in front of God and the rest of the restaurant witnesses, the whisker was extracted from my skin and glistening between the guy's thumb and finger. And I was richer.

out, damned spot!
or the day i discovered my
oven knobs come off

I couldn't stop staring at her oven knobs. Not because Beth is a bad conversationalist or anything. On that afternoon, she was telling me about her limited experience with geoduck, and she was serving sangria. She should have had my rapt attention. Instead, I kept glancing over at her oven, which happened to be the same GE XL44 as mine, with the same gray grills and lighted oven door. There was one distinct difference, however, which was what was so distracting: the knobs were clean. I was mystified as to how Beth kept them so immaculate because I knew she frequently slid casseroles in the oven, stirred full pots on the stovetop, and walked by the appliance holding drinks and other sloshy things in her hands. Beth has three teenage sons, and she's told me her food budget, which is impressively small; her family spends most nights at home eating something home-cooked, something the butcher had on sale. She isn't one of those annoying women on *House Hunters* who admits that she and her husband never cook but still absolutely *need* a double oven and restaurant-quality refrigerator for all the entertaining they do. The gleaming nature of Beth's oven knobs couldn't be blamed on lack of use.

I am—and I will tell you right now that this is a terrible way to be and I'm sorry and I will promise to try not to do it if I ever come to your house—the sort of houseguest who frequently notices the state of things like oven knobs. While I will not snoop through your medicine cabinet when I am in the bathroom, I might run my finger along the toilet-paper shelf to check for dust or peek behind the shower curtain to see if there are hard-water stains gunked up on the faucet. If there is dust or gunk, I will feel a faint glow of happiness—not because I've caught you in the act of Egregious Gunk Having, but because, in some small way, I will feel better about my own gunk, which often exists at nearly toxic levels—especially in the upstairs shower, which is used only by Scott and me. If there is no dust or gunk—and especially if the hostess was not expecting my visit or if she's said something along the lines of "Please excuse the mess"—I will think short, hateful thoughts about her and convince myself that she has a secret maid who wears camouflaged clothing and maybe a mask and who tiptoes into the house in the dead of night to tidy up a bit, unbeknownst to drop-in houseguests like me.

the knowledge that i am a subpar housekeeper used to give me a bit of pride.

Only one of my friends has admitted to having a maid, and only one of my friends has ever been employed as a maid, so while I understand that they do exist, I imagine them being very rare—like giant panda bears. Maids are also reserved for people who have "money saved for retirement" and an "emergency fund of at least six months' salary"—two responsible ideas that seem so ridiculously out of reach that I've stopped chastising myself for turning off the television whenever a financial expert starts discussing them. To me, having a maid is like having a tennis court on your roof garden. I've never even briefly considered hiring someone to take care of the mounds of dog hair collecting under the couch. Instead, I consider the social consequences of waxing my dog.

The knowledge that I am a subpar housekeeper used to give me a bit of pride. The feminist in me imagined myself throwing a scrubby brush into the fire in which other women had burned their bras. (I paid a lot of money for my bra, thank you very much. My scrubby brush, on the other hand, that's fodder for the fire if ever I've seen it.) Dish-soap and vacuum-cleaner commercials, in which women are either doing the work themselves or correcting the work their inadequate yet sharply dressed husbands have bumbled, made me indignant, and I'd often be caught yelling at the television if the voice-over addressed the advertisement to "Mom." I believed that my being an effective or even adequate vacuumer would somehow reinforce the nation's oppressive gender roles. It was better that I took the role of bumbling housekeeper. That would show 'em, sexist infidels!

When I got married after college, I promised myself I wouldn't be one of those women chained to her broom and dustpan—Scott and I would split the chores. Equally. But he would always take out the trash. (So what if I'm a fair-weather feminist? Trash is icky.) We tried a number of different tactics to divvy up duties: when the honor system didn't do the trick, we came up with a rotating system of lists that we taped to the refrigerator. Neither of us stuck to it. We just kind of *forgot* that toilets, unlike house cats, do not clean themselves; and we ignored the dishes in the sink until we absolutely needed to eat again.

We've gotten better at keeping up with the chores as we've gotten older—and especially since we've added babies, one of whom scoots around on her stomach. Nothing like a ten-month-old whose belly looks like the underside of a used Swiffer pad to motivate you to sweep. Most of the time, the house is generally clean and somewhat tidy and almost completely nontoxic—never as clean as my mother-in-law's house, though. I don't foresee myself ever becoming the type of person who can't go to sleep if there are dishes in the sink, or who puts her laundry away immediately, or who feels some compulsive need to scrub underneath her refrigerator once a month. But I would like for it to appear that I am.

Lately, feminist idealism has been trumped by the desire to avoid embarrassment over the state of my household. Oven knobs—like the tops of bookshelves, the dark corners beneath the end tables in the living room, and the underside of the refrigerator handle—fall in the category of Things I Usually Ignore but Now Must Take Care of Before My Mother or Mother-In-Law or Friend from Out of Town Comes to Visit. Objects with such intricate or awkwardly positioned parts seem too difficult for anyone to possibly keep clean. Likewise, because of their size and/or location, they typically go unnoticed by the casual dinner guest. I notice them frequently, however, and suspect that visitors of a long-term nature might, too. When my mother stayed with us for the weeks leading up to the birth of my first baby, for instance, I neglected the customary and very periodic attention I usually give to these places. She must have noticed because she entertained herself as we waited for the child by trying out the different attachments and features on the fancy vacuum cleaner that Scott and I store in the entryway closet. I forgave myself then because of the thirty-five-pound abdomen I'd developed.

At the risk of sounding like a guest on *The Montel Williams Show,* I blame my parents for this lackadaisical standard of cleanliness. They did most of the cleaning most of the time when I was growing up, and they did so with vigor and speed. I learned to rely on other people to take care of things, even if their methods didn't sync with my own. Dad did the vacuuming every morning. Throwing junk on the bed was his way of clearing a path for the Hoover. In high school, this technique irritated me; I had a methodical chaos going on in my bedroom that certainly shouldn't be disrupted by a parent with the organizational equivalent of a tornado. After he blew through, I carefully and precisely restored the unfolded clothes to their heap next to the closet; the makeup tray and hair dryer went back on the floor next to the mirror. I hated the quickness with which Dad "straightened up," and if I ever grew motivated enough to clean out my closet, I went about it in an entirely different manner.

Closet cleaning was a meticulous ordeal that included, among other things, emotive selections from a few Mariah

Carey cassettes and a nostalgic rereading of all the old love letters I'd collected in the shoe box on the top shelf. A good cleaning of the closet usually dragged on for days, as I'd grow lethargic and slow after reorganizing the Barbie shoes that were still stashed in the Barbie case that hadn't been played with for years. I guess I thought someday there might be money in those oft-used dolls, so it was imperative that the shoes be organized. Usually, I got tired of cleaning after a day or so and impatiently shoved the somewhat-more-organized contents back into their dimly lit cave of disorder. The Barbie shoes were clearly in better order, but the tangle of blouses that prevented the door from closing remained as disheveled and as de-shelved as ever.

I still clean like that. Which brings me back to the oven knobs. After returning home from Beth's, I went directly to my oven. I looked it over, and, sure enough, could barely make out the tick marks that helped me distinguish between "low" and "high." I got out a washcloth. Then a sponge. Then a tooth-brush. After fifteen minutes of scrubbing, I could still see the ring of dirt under the knob—a now very pronounced line that indicated exactly how far the toothbrush would reach. Frustrated, I pulled on the offending knob. Just like that it popped off into my hand.

It was the kind of win I needed to continue. I scrubbed for more than two hours. While the knobs were bathing in a pool of chemically enhanced warm water, I pulled the oven away from the wall to wipe down the back and sweep underneath, I soaked the drip pans, I finally used the self-cleaning feature that I had heard so much about. I got into the tiny crevices that had, up to that point, eluded me. In short, I wore myself out. But the stovetop gleamed. When I went to bed that night, I felt shiny and un-spaghetti-sauced. The rest of the house still had its problems, but I felt a distinct feeling of joy that *one thing* was just right.

The experience reminded me of Benjamin Franklin's quest for moral perfection. His autobiography chronicles his attempt to "live without committing any fault at any time." Those founding fathers knew how to set a goal. To do it, he made a chart that consisted of the thirteen virtues he thought neces- sary to attaining moral perfection. That's doable, right? Thir- teen virtues? I can kick the asses of thirteen virtues! Maybe. Then you read one like the last one on his chart: "Humility: Imitate Jesus and Socrates." Maybe not.

Franklin was nothing if not determined. He attempted to conquer and perfect each virtue, one at a time: "I made a little book in which I allotted a page for each of the virtues. I ruled each page with red ink so as to have seven col- umns, one for each day of the week, marking each column with thirteen red lines, marking the beginning of each line with the first letter of one of the virtues, on which line in its proper column I might mark by a little black spot every fault I found upon examination to have been committed respecting that virtue upon that day." Easy peasy. After a week of con- centrating on, say, Temperance, the virtue would become habitual, instinctual, almost an unconscious motor skill, and he'd be free to focus on something else, like being Jesus or

the stovetop gleamed. when i went to bed that night, i felt shiny and un-spaghetti- sauced.

Socrates. So the oven was my First Virtue of Cleanliness. If I could keep it clean for a week, I could move on to something else, maybe the sink, and my house would eventually become the picture of sanitized perfection.

Franklin never became morally perfect, a fact that his contraction of syphilis is probably indicative of. And the next night, when enchilada sauce bubbled all over my sparkling stovetop, I realized my quest for a perfectly maintained kitchen would be more difficult than I had anticipated. I railed at the offending sauce. I fell to my knees, wringing my red, sauce-stained hands toward heaven like a crazed Lady Macbeth. No, I didn't. But I considered it. The hours of scrubbing the night before seemed like a black hole of wasted time, much like making the bed in the morning. I was actually going to have to get out the sponge AGAIN.

The Catholic tradition of confession has never made much sense to me. I've wondered how Catholics keep track of all the sins they've committed since last confession. Even if you're a good Catholic who confesses regularly, the job seems daunting. I'd constantly worry that I'd forgotten something vital—something like thinking murderous thoughts about the slow check writer in front of me in line at the grocery store. What then? Hell for sure? I can't help but think it would just be easier to use a blanket confession: "I've done lots of stuff wrong. Please forgive me for everything I've ever done and ever will do. Or think. Or not do. Or consider. To anyone.

if a sheet is untucked in a forest with no one there to see it, is it really untucked?

About anyone. Ever." There probably aren't too many priests who would accept such a confession, although my knowledge of what happens at confession comes mainly from mobster movies, so I could be wrong. Regardless, confession is probably one of the more repetitive tasks for Catholics. They must find themselves apologizing repeatedly for the same offenses, probably using many of the same words. Like the habitual snorer, most of us can't seem to cease our crimes altogether, as sinning seems to be more of an unconscious motor skill than not sinning.

Confession is like bed making when you consider the task's slow and deliberate repetition. Tucking the sheets. Smoothing the comforter. Plumping the pillows. It's work that should be done daily, or at least as often as the untucking, the crumpling, and the smooshing occur. My resistance to confession probably comes from the same place as my resistance to making the bed: doing something that I know with certainty I will have to do again soon. Over and over again, until I am too old or weak or sick to do it or until my children are old enough to take over doing all the unpleasant household tasks. (Don't tell Miles or Genevieve, but the option to delegate the worst chores to our offspring was high up on Scott's and my list of Reasons to Have Children.) There is also the matter of enforcement to consider. None exists. No one knows or cares or sees that my bed is unmade, no one knows or cares or sees that my confessions are unsaid, and if a sheet is untucked in a forest with no one there to see it, is it really untucked?

The monastic tradition has a much different outlook on work. As Joan Chittister notes in *The Rule of Benedict:*

Insights for the Ages, work and prayer go together in the Benedictine order: "One focuses the skills of the body on the task
of co-creation. The other focuses the gifts of the mind on the
lessons of the heart. One without the other is not Benedictine
spirituality." To think of housework in tandem with prayer is
difficult for someone like me, who will resort to cleaning up
only when there is writing to be done. It makes sense, though.
With washing and scouring comes a certain focused discipline.
With the repetition of folding and tucking comes a quietness
of heart. The moving of one's hands in the direction of order
can inexplicably result in an appreciation for the beauty, the
calm, the absolute value of the present moment.

I am learning to drive a stick shift, which is an irritating thing
to attempt after you've been driving a car for more than a
dozen years. I don't like having my brain completely occupied
with the task of driving; there isn't room for anything other
than "Do I shift now? Clutch? No clutch?" My left foot and
right hand used to sit idly by. Now they are involved in the
action, and I can't say they're happy about it.

Scott tried to teach me back in college, but it was after
we'd been dating long enough that I couldn't stand him teaching me anything, so, nearly a decade later, the job fell to my
dad. We went out to an abandoned parking lot and literally
drove in circles for hours. The same motions, over and over
again, until left foot and right hand knew what to do. Dad said
he knew I was getting the hang of it when I started telling him
a story about something new the baby was doing.

"You can shift gears without having to concentrate on it," he said. "That's progress."

So the circles paid off. The muscles in my extremities began to anticipate how hard I needed to push the gas and when to shift into a different gear, the unconscious parts of my brain took over for the conscious ones, and I could talk and think about something else. Room in my crowded mind opened up. This also happened when I learned to type and play the guitar. I could do something that I couldn't do before, but it took time and some practice, repetition that at first seemed like such a waste of time.

The repetition inherent in Franklin's virtue charts didn't make him perfect. Maybe it made him better, or at least more aware of his faults, but definitely not perfect. Sometimes the gears still grind. So what do we do with a biblical command like Jesus' "Be perfect, therefore, as your heavenly Father is perfect"? The notion that one should even attempt perfection is laughable when it comes from Benjamin Franklin but not as easily shrugged off when it comes from Jesus.

Luckily, as Kathleen Norris points out, the word, as used in the New Testament, is "not a scary word, so much as a scary translation." In the Latin, Norris explains, the meaning is closer to "complete," "whole," or "full-grown." Not "without blemish or stain." Emphasis, then, falls upon growth. The struggle for perfection requires a process, perhaps a lifelong one, that eventually, with lots of grace along the way, results in maturity. Completeness. Maybe perfection is not even as dependent on the moral as we sometimes assume. What we do counts, but if perfection is wholeness, it seems to be more a matter of being than a matter of doing.

Today, my oven knobs are clean. They are rusted a bit underneath, and the markings have begun to fade and chip from the rough sides of years of sponges. They are not quite as shiny as they once were, but learning how to maintain them has kept me from replacing either them, or worse, the entire oven. Cleaning up the spilled sauces—spaghetti, barbecue, white wine, Alfredo—requires patience, forgiveness, self-discipline, and, most of all, grace—all in little increments, of course. A stovetop is a very small thing, but it, too, is a matter of infinite hope.

Easter

but dairy cows
already knew this

I was in the midst of graduate school at the University of Kansas when my son was born in July, convinced that nursing was the right way to go—that "Breast Is Best"—mostly because Scott and I were broke and cheap. It was a nice surprise that there seemed to be a nutritional and developmental bonus for our frugality, and we were determined not to buy an ounce of formula for the first year of Miles's life.

Early on, breast-feeding was relatively easy. Miles never had problems latching, and my milk supply was bountiful. I tried to enjoy nursing, and most of the time I could. I also learned to do a variety of things one-handed, like reading a book, eating meals, and using the television remote. (Okay, that last one has always been a one-handed task, but I needed a longer list, and it turns out that breast-feeding didn't really teach me any marketable skills or cool party tricks.)

Then in August, I started school again.

Not to be dissuaded, I bought a used breast pump from a friend who was finished breast-feeding children. I should have been tipped off by the maniacal smile on her face, the way she seemed to believe that this moment—the handing off of the breast pump—was more worthy of celebration than having the babies, but I wasn't. I had no idea what was in store for me until the next morning when I attempted to strap that thing on.

Two funnelly cups. Check. Two tubes, purchased new to avoid funky sharing-of-the-breast-pump germs that may or may not exist, depending on how much you trust the Medela company to tell the truth regardless of profit margins. Check. A bra that a dominatrix would be proud of (were it not bright white with scalloped edges) with holes cut out for your nipples to pop through—perfect for a hands-free pumping experience. Check. Two tiny rubbery things referred to in the instruction manual as "membranes." Gross, but: Check. Everything was accounted for. That first day, I spent a good twenty minutes configuring where membranes and funnels should go, flipping switches and turning knobs, listening as the suck-and-blow sound—the one that would become so familiar over the course of that first year—sped up and slowed down with each adjustment. The process seemed sort of neat. I'd been somewhat excited when registering for the breast-pump accessories, like I was with any other new baby toy, and I'd waited with anticipation for the first time I'd get to try them out.

I quickly discovered that using a breast pump is not really that neat. But dairy cows already knew this.

Taking the breast pump with you to various outside-the-home commitments like graduate school is even less neat. The University of Kansas is situated atop Mount Oread, which is affectionately nicknamed "The Hill." On my very first day of

classes, even though I knew how desperate the parking situation on campus is, I came to school in the highest heels I owned
with my laptop case slung over one shoulder. By the end of the
twenty-minute uphill hike, the makeup I'd agonized over was
dripping down my face in the August sun, and my shoes were
wearing indentations into my feet. The breast pump, and all of
its bazillion required accoutrements, made this hike even more
awkward. I identified with the T-shirts someone in the freshman class had designed that pictured a stick figure ascending
a forty-five-degree angle. HILL, NO! it read.

Laptop, lunch sack, stack of student work, jacket, school-
bag, breast pump. All of the various items hanging from me
seemed essential for each day's work. Of
course, the eighteen- and nineteen-year-old
women that populated the campus didn't
sympathize. They, with their oversized purses
that functioned like undersized backpacks,
couldn't imagine what one might need besides
a thin spiral notebook, a phone, and perhaps a
spare lipstick. I tried not to begrudge these
nameless undergraduates the freedom that
comes with being young. I tried to remember
that I had been there once. That I wasn't lug-

*i quickly dis-
covered that
using a breast
pump is not
really that
neat. but dairy
cows already
knew this.*

ging around breast pumps with me as an undergraduate either.
But sometimes I couldn't help it. So I made an internal list of
the witty and clever retorts I would hurl in the unlikely event
that one of them was ever to question me regarding my pleth-
ora of bags. This self-righteous indignation made me feel a
tiny bit better. Then I'd arrange the straps of all the bags to

avoid crushing my bloated breasts, and I would trudge, heavy-laden, up the hill every Tuesday and Thursday morning.

At least I had an office. Situated at the end of a dark hallway that one of my students christened "Grad Land," the office was small, windowless, and shared with two other graduate students. Not exactly a corner suite with a view of Wall Street. The three of us had tried to make the place look more cheerful: we put up a few posters—left over from our undergraduate days—set out a coffeepot, and moved in a small refrigerator. But the office never lost its cold feeling or musty smell, probably because the entire English department is located in Wescoe Hall, a converted parking garage that is, quite certainly, the ugliest building on campus and, almost as certainly, chock-full of mold that was allegedly making some longtime professors sick. Even though it wouldn't win any architectural or interior design awards, the office was at least a place to store and use the breast pump without having to haul it hither and yon to every department meeting or class session. I've heard of women who've had to pump in their cars or in the stalls of public restrooms. That must be worse than creating a "Do Not Disturb" sign on a Post-it for your office door, contemplating whether you should add PUMPING IN PROGRESS to halfway explain the sounds of the machine. These sounds were always strange, but somehow stranger still in the hallowed and thin walls of higher education. Despite the efforts of academia to be as accepting and progressive as possible, newborns are still a group often feared and "othered" (to coin a collegiate term) in the college setting. It might, in fact, be the only place I took Miles as an infant where he was looked at more as a consequence of careless behavior than anything else.

What made the situation bearable was that my officemate was breast-feeding during the same time period. During our forty-five-minute lunch break, we'd hurriedly strap ourselves up to our respective pumps, politely turn toward opposing walls, and discuss our lesson plans as her machine pumped and mine sucked. The ultimate height of professionalism. I never had a student knock on the door during these pumping sessions (I'm sure the blunt nature of the Post-it was a deterrent), but the male colleague who was the third occupant of Wescoe 2008 often had to retreat to some corner of the building until he was sure that the breast pumps were safely stored under our desks and that the freshly expressed milk was chilling near some ice packs in the insulated pouches of our carrying cases.

During those months, I complained regularly to Scott, my carpool companion, my mother, my friends, and my officemates about the indignities and hassles of balancing a baby and a professional career. I grumbled out curse words when the strap of the "stylish" carrying case of my breast pump would slip off my shoulder on the walk up The Hill, or when I stood at my closet in the morning, unable to wear half my wardrobe because either nursing bras looked funny under the tight or sheer or halfway-non-granny-looking fabric, or there was no way to gain easy entry for pumping. I hated the restrictions the pump, and therefore the child, put on me. But I didn't yet realize that physically carrying around the device would be only among the first (and not nearly the most difficult) sacrifices I'd make for my child. But as most mothers do, I knew even then, when Miles was only a few months old and still gagging on his own tongue, that he was worth the hassle.

Being attached to either a baby or a breast pump every three hours got me thinking about the nature of dependence. In America, it's easy to believe that being dependent is something to avoid. We have always appreciated independence—our forefathers made it one of their top priorities, finishing their work on the Declaration of Independence just in time to celebrate the first Independence Day. Since then, American writers, artists, reality-television stars, ad executives, and people with too many firecrackers and not enough brain cells have celebrated independence as the best sort of virtue. Besides, dependent people are those pathetic teens who always need a boyfriend or girlfriend or the addicts who can't get away from whatever it is that's causing them so much harm or that guy who still lives in his parents' house and meets his Dungeons & Dragons focus group weekly at the local Panera Bread. Nobody wants to be *that* guy, unless you happen to be that guy. And if you are that guy, rest assured that you probably already make more money than I do, and if you don't, you will someday.

being attached to either a baby or a breast pump every three hours got me thinking about the nature of dependence.

But any parent will tell you that we all enter the world completely dependent upon other human beings. The magnitude of this realization hit me hard in those first months of being a mother. When that little human began to understand that I was the one to go to for comfort, a familiar smell, the right way to hold him to rock him to sleep, and, perhaps most importantly, food, I couldn't help but enjoy the feeling of being needed so intensely. Later, of course, that feeling wears off. But back then, this somewhat obvious realization was pretty amazing: Miles could do almost nothing by himself. He needed Scott and me absolutely.

he always goes, because he is a good person, and because i remind him of the "in sickness and in health" part of the vows he took.

Childhood is not the only period of dependency we encounter during our lifetimes. I think about this whenever I get sick, as I am the pathetic sort of sick person who wishes her mother would fly in from California whenever I have a sore throat because she knows the right kind of Lipton chicken-noodle packet soup to buy. I groggily, weakly, pitifully beg Scott to go to the store for a different cold medicine or maybe some tasteless crackers. He always goes, because he is a good person, and because I remind him of the "in sickness and in health" part of the vows he took. Before *God* and everyone. And usually around this time, I, hopped up on Sudafed, consider how awful it would be not to have someone to run to the store.

This happened to me only once, when Scott was away on a church mission trip and I contracted the worst flu I've ever had—during the summer. I decided to watch *The Stand*, not knowing that that movie is the worst thing to watch when you're dreadfully sick and it's really hot outside, as the circumstances mirror your life in very disturbing ways. I survived the sickness, but only barely. And I think a few people at the grocery store expected my face to start melting off when I finally made it out of the apartment, unkempt and in sweatpants, to buy some much-needed provisions.

The most basic and necessary human activities teach us that we can't go it alone—at our most vulnerable we need other people to help us eat, bathe, move, sometimes even breathe. We need this when we are very young, very old, very sick, very poor, very sad—and these vulnerable states happen more often than most of us like to admit. The first time I saw my dad like this—he had an extreme case of vertigo, probably from spray-painting a car in our less-than-ventilated garage without a mask—I was already a college sophomore. For most of my life, I half expected that he'd live forever. Not because I'm that stupid but because he was that tough. He walked around barefoot most of the time, bringing shoes with him only so he could walk into the Kmart without violating their highly classy "No Shoes, No Shirt, No Service" policy. Seeing him resigned to his bed, barely able to open his eyes from the dizziness, was a new experience for me. It was the first time my dad really needed anything from me and the first time I really took care of him.

The miracle of it all is that people help. More than that, they want to. "Man is a sacrificial being," wrote Orthodox theologian Alexander Schmemann, "because he finds his life in love, and love is sacrificial: it puts the value, the very meaning of life in the other and gives life to the other, and in this giving, in his sacrifice, finds the meaning and joy of life."[1] What a beautiful thought, especially when most of what we hear about the nature of humanity—on the news, in movies, on the signs of religious zealots at football games, from each other—has to do with the intrinsic evil that we're born with. It helps to recognize that there are parts of us that *are* pure, sacrificial, and good. That most of us spend a good part of our lives caring for and feeding those we're closest to. As Sara Miles writes in *Take this Bread,* "People feed one another constantly from their own bodies, their own plates, their own inadequate stores of insufficient food. Food is what people have in common, and it is, precisely, common."[2]

The sacrificial nature of sharing food is one reason why the act of taking Communion is so important to the church. We break bread together, sharing what we have, pausing for a moment to partake in something common—the eating of food—and reflecting also on how uncommon the act of communing together can be.

At my church, we serve Communion every Sunday. There are usually four people who serve, and Bill is often one of them. He's my favorite one to watch. Bill is why the word *hulking* exists, and he looks something like I imagine a Viking to have looked—except he usually wears Nike tennis shoes, and probably the Vikings had sturdier shoes. But whenever he serves, it's not the least bit awkward even though most of the rest of the congregation is significantly less hulking than Bill.

Our tradition is to have people come to the front to receive Communion, and letting people decide to stand up and walk somewhere, on their own, in the middle of a church service, is a surefire way to ensure that someone will do it wrong. You can hardly blame them when each congregation does Communion differently. My friend Shawna, who has been going to churches for her entire life, once got to the front of the Communion line at a new church and wrested the cup from a surprised server to take a few gulps of the Savior's Blood before realizing that no, no one else was drinking from the actual cup and yes, everyone else was delicately dipping their crackers and returning to their seats. I tried to tell her that the Communion instructions are among the most important parts of the service to PAY ATTENTION TO, if only to avoid looking like a fool, but Shawna still maintains that her mistake was practically unavoidable, what with the biggish guy in front of her impeding her view of how everybody else was doing it.

But Bill, somehow, seems to anticipate and sidestep all of the things that might go wrong with Communion. If someone is on crutches, he positions the plate and the cup nearest their free hand so they can easily reach the elements. If someone is young or short, he leans over to their level, which is sometimes half his own height, so that they don't have to reach. Old people or those in wheelchairs who have a hard time making it up to the Communion server are given at-their-seat service without having to ask. And if someone comes up too early or to the wrong place, he swoops in so quickly that people don't even realize they've made a mistake and nobody ends up looking foolish. I imagine that, if we're given jobs in heaven,

Bill's will be to serve Communion. And his line will always go smoothly.

The word *communion*—along with the other English words *commonality* and *community*—is derived from the Greek root *koinon-*. That these three words share a root is not surprising to anyone who has studied language, and that these three words share a meaning is not surprising to anyone who has studied Christianity. The word *koinonia,* which is used most often in Paul's letters, has a variety of different meanings including "association," "communion," "fellowship," and "close relationship." And although the Greek word was not one known to Jesus or really ever used in the Gospels, the idea was both present and vitally important. So while each church may have a different way of distributing Communion, the underlying idea is that the activity is one that unifies and characterizes our participation in the larger body of Christ (both personally and corporately), which often seems fragmented and disparate in today's very denominationalized world.

Much has been written about the importance of Communion to the church. I don't understand most of it, neither do I want to attempt to explain the theological intricacies of what people say and believe about the Eucharist, about whether the wine (or, if you're a nervous Protestant, the grape Juicy Juice) and the bread are transformed somehow into the very body and blood of Christ. Still, the act itself is one of my favorite parts of a church service, and not just because I can giggle at other people's idiosyncrasies. When I think about what Communion must have meant the very first time, when Jesus and his disciples were eating together just prior to his death on the cross, I can't help but feel struck by how ordinary it must have all seemed. We're just eating. Together. Even the remembering part—when Jesus takes the bread, breaks it, and says, "Do this in remembrance of me"—doesn't sound weird or overly sanctimonious the way some people tend to read it. It sounds to me like he's saying, "Remember me when you're together and you're having bread." So at church, even though the act of going forward and choosing a tiny piece of bread from a tray, and trying your best not to drip grape juice on the server's hand as you move the tiny bread from the cup to your mouth is a little bit weird and sometimes even overly sanctimonious, I like to think about how we're just eating. Together. And the remembering part comes easily.

when i think about what that first communion with jesus must have meant, i can't help but feel struck by how ordinary it must have all seemed.

This is not to say that taking Communion, or more specifically, remembering Christ, comes without challenge. In fact, the less we remember about Christ and the more we invent about him, the easier it is to follow him because he begins to seem more and more like the person inventing him and less and less like the radical reformer and savior that he was. I think about this sometimes when I get hung up on praying for things akin to superhuman powers: "Lord, protect me and my family. Give us good health, strength, the ability to leap tall buildings in a single bound. And also, a Go-Go-Gadget Arm would be helpful when I forget to bring the TV remote with me to the couch." I am praying this to a person who willingly carried his cross to a death that was both undeserved and something he could have easily prevented. To a person who was so sacrificial that, as he died, he was praying for the people killing him. Remembering becomes even more of a challenge when we strive to have what theologian John Zizioulas describes as a "memory of the future," which basically means transcending the linear idea of time we're so comfortable with and embracing the idea that Christ is in all—past, present, and future. If we limit our remembering to only what Christ did while walking on the earth, how can we possibly fully appreciate the Second Coming? And what about Christ's presence now? How in the world might we "remember" that?

My friend Maria has had a long history with depression, and she was dealing with it again after she experienced a sudden miscarriage. In order to help her through it, I did the only thing I could think of: I brought food. Grocery bags full of the fixings for fish tacos, to be precise. I planned to spend the evening cooking for the family, helping with the house and the kids so Maria and her husband could have a bit of peace. It would be like if Paula Deen and Mother Teresa teamed up.

When I arrived at Maria's that afternoon, the atmosphere felt different. Usually, there are choo-choo trains strewn around the couch and library books stacked up on the dining room table—the house has the wonderful feeling of being perpetually in midplay. That day, although the trains and the books were still strewn about, they seemed less buoyant; laundry and dishes and stale air were more prevalent, and Maria was in the bathroom, crying. And just so you know, it is way easier to help your friends when they entertain you with their sarcastic wit and delicious margaritas than when they are inconsolable and weary. So I blame her.

When her twin boys got home from kindergarten, they were fighting—loudly and obnoxiously. And loudly. Most of the time, they get home with funny questions and surprising anecdotes about other kids in their class. This was not at all how things would go for Paula Deen, and I spent more of my energy trying to coax the boys into better moods than I did adding butter to anything. Her baby girl wouldn't stop crying. The oven was broken. When Maria's husband got home, I had to ask him to cook the fish on the grill outside. You know, as a relaxing way to end a stressful day at work and an emotionally haggard week, why don't you cook the dinner that I was going to cook for you? My plans to care for Maria and her family that night were slowly unraveling.

By the time the food was finally on the table—an hour or so later than planned—we were all exhausted. We sat around the table, staring at each other with blank looks. The boys—who, I'll have you know, are known to eat weird things like shiitake mushrooms and quinoa and tofu—wouldn't eat the fish. The baby was still crying. But still, somehow, the food helped.

The phrase *body of Christ* is used in the Bible in three major ways—Jesus uses it to describe the bread broken in Communion, Paul uses it to describe the Church and how it should function, and, of course, the phrase denotes Jesus' actual, physical body. The one he used to eat and drink with the tax collectors, to walk among Gentiles and Jews, to die on the cross. Understanding this threefold meaning is vital, I think, to understanding our calling: to "feed one another constantly from [our] own bodies, [our] own plates, [our] own inadequate stores of insufficient food." It is easy with those we love the most, and I remember this now when I take Communion—holding Genevieve, a second beautiful child, one who will receive the elements secondhand, through my own body. A miracle on many levels. It is harder to share food with a stranger, harder still with an enemy. Or people who double-dip. Or someone who insists on using the phrase *booya* without even a touch of irony. But that is what we, the Church, are meant to do.

Maria needed to be served Communion, I think. But more than that—and intrinsic in the act of "doing" Communion at all—she needed to "sit at the table," as they say. She needed fellowship and community and friends who might act as the very hands of Christ to her. We all do. In the same sense, I needed to serve her Communion, needed to remember Christ yesterday, tomorrow, and yes, today. Eating together, in this sense, is extraordinary and sacrificial and pure and good, even when the oven is broken and the kids are crying and you're all in really bad moods.

Hill, yes.

a sprinkling

At a former church of mine, it was tradition that every Palm Sunday the pastor would dip a palm frond in water, wave it overhead, and spray a fine mist over the congregation. "Remember your baptism!" he would always proclaim. It was a lovely tradition, I think, and a great way to kick off Holy Week.

Pastor Greg was an interim guy, so he'd never done the dipping and spraying before, but he was also a traditionalist who took great joy in rituals like these. Greg was from a small town in Tennessee, and you'd never guess, either by his accent or his wardrobe (some of which was shiny), that he belonged behind the pulpit. He'd often line up his shirt buttons incorrectly, and when he lifted the bread and the cup for Communion, it was not an oddity to glimpse his somewhat hairy belly button peeking from beneath his shirt. On Greg's first Palm Sunday as pastor, he dipped the palm frond in the water. With a vengeance, holy or otherwise, he launched the water at the congregation.

Unfortunately, Greg had dipped the frond too deeply or perhaps had flung it with a bit too much abandon, and my friend Diane's parents, who were visiting from Michigan and sitting in the front row, were doused with so much water that her curls went flat and his tie clung to his shirt like a limp sardine. They spent the rest of that sermon remembering their baptisms, I suspect.

Baptism, for Christians, is a re-creation of the Easter miracle. Everything from the dying to sins to the rising again, it is a minipicture of arguably the most important miracle ever to have taken place. But before it was that, baptism was a purification ritual. People would be baptized over and over again, the "bath" or "wash" a method of acknowledging sinfulness and symbolically purifying themselves. It was, in a sense, a way to get closer to God, but it had to be repeated again and again; the purification was never complete. When Christ came and died, the symbolic significance of baptism changed, and now believers are baptized once: a sort of entrance into a community of faith. It's seen as a way to identify ourselves, even unify ourselves, with the death, burial, and resurrection of Christ.

I was baptized when I was fourteen years old, at a church event at our friends' pool. I remember being preoccupied with how plain I looked. I would be standing in front of everyone with no makeup on and bangs that were neither curled nor hairsprayed. I remember wondering if the T-shirt I'd worn over my bathing suit would be too see-through or clingy after it got wet. As Anne Lamott writes, "Most of what we do in worldly life is geared toward our staying dry, looking good, not going under. But in baptism, in lakes and rain and tanks and fonts, you agree to something that's a little sloppy because at the same time it's also holy, and absurd."[1] I guess I really was entering into the community, even if I was somewhat begrudging my lack of styling products. I remember wondering if I'd feel different after I was baptized; most of my friends had had the experience as infants, or at least as young children, and couldn't remember at all what they'd felt. What I understood of how my pastors spoke about baptism was sometimes reminiscent of a rite of passage. You weren't really "in" unless you were baptized, and though I'd felt "in" for as long as I could remember, I couldn't help wondering if maybe I had just been deluding myself.

After I was dunked (sprinkling was for wimps, my church must have believed), I felt good. My friends and family applauded from deck chairs, and I think there was some singing.

My soggy bangs and sopping T-shirt were not the problems I had anticipated them to be. But as far as feeling different, I can't say that I did.

When Miles was baptized as an infant, twenty or so years later, I wondered anew if I'd notice anything different about him. I was certainly more able to understand and explain the symbolic significance of the act at this point in my life. Maybe this time the experience would be more profoundly affecting. But again, though the service was nice and though I cried at this event just as I'm sure I'll cry at important events in Miles's life to come, I couldn't really detect a change in him after the sprinkles (dunking was for show-offs, my church must have believed).

Baptism, as symbols go, is a beautiful one. Though I have no theological reason for it, the writer in me prefers the dunking method. There's something about the way a person is plunged into a pool, or better yet, an ocean or river, that conjures up a picture of dying to the old, sinful nature. It's a quick act, lasting no more than a few seconds (contrary to my naïve fear that maybe I'd run out of breath and drown during my own baptism). The water has just enough time to rush around a person, wrapping itself around every strand of hair and sliding under every last fingernail. Then, up. Air. Light. Sunshine.

It seems only right that baptism happens in the water—the element that Saint Teresa described as one of which she was "so fond." Water has symbolized such a variety of concepts and ideas, in the Bible and elsewhere, that it's difficult to keep track: chaos and peace, renewal and stagnation, eternal life and certain death. It is the most natural of elements, one we depend on daily, and one that can only be "created" by human beings with the right molecules and certain pieces of equipment and circumstances. Even then, the quantities would not be large enough to sustain life if water didn't continue falling from the sky in droplets, in flakes, in chunks, or bubbling up in rivers and lakes, drifting in with the sunrise as the morning dew. Water is a miraculous wonder. We don't appreciate water fully, I imagine, because we're so used to it coming painlessly from faucets, showerheads, and hose bibs; however, it seems impossible to ignore the importance of water entirely, and though I may not know "thirst" the way some cultures and people do, I still find much to marvel at.

In the first months of my second pregnancy, the only place I could escape from the responsibilities associated with the first child and the morning sickness associated with the second was in the shower. Conservation and high utility bills be damned, I would stand under the steady stream of the hottest water I could endure for a good half hour without guilt. The white noise of the spray, the heavy fog in the room, the heat and gentle massage of the water was enough to make me feel alone for a moment, which for a mother is a precious thing indeed. Well worth the cost. As the water trickled down my body, the warmth was immediate and enveloping. I was reminded of these moments later on in the pregnancy, when the swimming pool was the only place I could jump or maneuver with much energy; I felt buoyed by the water, like a fragile, bulbous glass whale protected on all sides with liquid packing peanuts. And I remembered it again when I was giving birth in a tub of water, which my nurse told me is often referred to as "the midwife's epidural." It helped the pain of labor and seemed to relax my aching muscles and skin.

the water has just enough time to rush around a person, wrapping itself around every strand of hair and sliding under every last fingernail.

Perhaps it was our family trips to the lake during my childhood that taught me to seek refuge in the water. Vacations were never easy for the five of us—Mom was usually distracted with packing the lunch and everybody's suitcases, Dad was distracted with leaving on time and getting all the packed suitcases strapped to the hood of the car, and my siblings and I were distracted by the fact that there was no teleportation device, and we would, indeed, have to suffer the two-hour car ride to get there. Our little motorboat was usually hitched hap-hazardly to the back of the car, a car that was not built for hauling boats, so we never made good time. Dad would keep one eye on the road and one on the swaying mass behind us. To his credit, we never lost the boat, and in all honesty, I never worried we would.

It was during these summer trips that I learned to knee-board. The memory seems almost like a fabrication now because I've grown out of this skill just as utterly as I've grown out of my fifth-grade bathing suit. Even the thought of jump-ing in a lake behind a boat makes the languid, timid, almost-middle-aged woman I've become long for a copy of *People* magazine, a fuzzy towel, and a giant pair of sunglasses. I am more of a languisher than a boarder anymore. But back then, I lived for my turn to hit the water. I remember the slow pull of the boat starting up, how I'd have to hold on to the handles with all my strength for those first crucial seconds, and then, like magic, I'd be skimming across the water like a skipped stone. It was like flying, and all I could think about was the sound the wind made in my ears.

In some biblical passages, baptism is spoken about as a new birth, and this ties the act to Easter. As theologian N. T. Wright explains, "Jesus's resurrection is directly instrumen-tal in bringing about this new birth and its consequences. It is all because of what happened at Easter: a new reality has opened up in the world, a new kind of life both inward and, importantly, outward in holiness and in the hope of our own resurrection."[2] Wright is my kind of theologian. In his book

Surprised by Hope, he advocates for the Easter season to become a sort of eight-day party for the church with champagne before morning prayers and lots of whooping and carrying on at church. He's right, I think, when he talks about how adept the Christian church is at celebrating the forty days of Lent—the mourning, the focus on sins and death. We do Lent up good. But Easter, on the other hand, comes and goes with maybe an upbeat hymn or two to mark its passage. (And a few Reese's eggs in your Easter basket, which, I'll give you, is something of a celebration.) That's it. How sad that our great festival—our celebration of Christ risen—has turned into an afterthought. Or that we've so thoroughly forgotten how good champagne can taste after a fast.

If I'm honest, witnessing—and even experiencing—the baptismal act has been less than impacting for me. When Pastor Greg whisked his giant palm frond at me on that Palm Sunday, most of what I remembered was past experiences with wet hair. And most of what I remember about that remembering was Diane's mother's wet hair. Although I do appreciate the beauty of the symbolism in being baptized, that alone has never seemed to be enough. I suppose that some part of me wants to see doves, like at Jesus' baptism, or perhaps tiny, singing angels descending from the heavens and landing on the baptized person—something a little bit fantastic to mark the momentous nature of the occasion. But usually there's nothing but water.

One thing I've come to discover over years of faith is that usually God doesn't bend his divine will to make things flashier for me. Even though I tend to enjoy tiny, singing angels,

God has decided their efforts are better utilized elsewhere. In any case, Wright is blunt in his agreement that baptism is not meant to be showy. He offers an entirely different way of reading the event: "Baptism is not magic, a conjuring trick with water. But neither is it simply a visual aid. It is one of the points, established by Jesus himself, where heaven and earth interlock, where new creation, resurrection life, appears within the midst of the old."[3] (So actually his idea is even flashier than mine, which is a nice turn of events.) His explanation also makes it clear that baptism is a place where God draws near, the term *interlocking* meaning "to fit into each other, as parts of machinery, so that all action is synchronized."[4]

one thing i've come to discover over years of faith is that usually god doesn't bend his divine will to make things flashier for me.

My favorite part about the story of the resurrection, as it is told in the Gospels, is what happened to the temple veil. Call me a sucker for significant detail, but this seems to get at God's essential nature, of his appreciation for irony, and his pure prowess in making the dismal beautiful and poignant. The temple veil— by many accounts thirty-by-sixty feet in height and length, a handbreadth in thickness, and woven of seventy-two twisted plaits each consisting of twenty-four threads—was the curtain that divided the holy place of more routine temple gatherings from the "holy of holies." Only the high priest was allowed entrance into this holiest of places, and only once a year to quickly offer the blood of an atoning sacrifice for Israel. Then he'd have to skedaddle. The veil, which took three hundred priests to manipulate, is said to have torn clean through on the day of Jesus' death on the cross. It was the first time in a very long time that there was absolutely no separation from the holy of holies—not only from the room but from the very presence of God.

Although many spiritual writers have written volumes on the ramifications of the resurrection and the tearing of the temple veil, I know of no greater miracle than the chance to be nearer to Christ—no longer separated by a curtain, a status, a sin. We hear echoes of Wright's description of baptism in the way that he writes of the spiral of events since the cross: "The created order, which God has begun to redeem in the resurrection of Jesus, is a world in which heaven and earth are designed not to be separated but to come together."[5] I've always believed that our primary human longing is for nearness—to each other and to God. What an example of grace—that he might go to death to bring us near, to rip down metaphysical walls and physical veils. His resurrection was the first step, Wright maintains, and our instruction, from the Great Commission onward, is to be grace to each other: to be near and to spread the good news of God's nearness to the world.

One summer day when I was eight years old, my cousins, brother, and I found ourselves fascinated by a garden hose. My dad was only using it to spray down the driveway. Usually his work didn't interrupt our play. Usually we didn't even notice the hose or the nozzle that attached to the top and controlled the strength and trajectory of the spray. But by some accident, my young cousin Kayla stepped on the sprayer, the spout pointing up, and a sprinkler effect occurred. The trigger was old and rusty, so the spray went on for a good twenty seconds, stuck in the "on" position until it slowly squeaked back to resting. I remember dropping everything to come and see the mist that shot up like a geyser and drenched a surprised Kayla.

When the water stopped, my brother Hutch thought it would be fun to try the trick again. He sneaked up to the sprayer and tapped it with one brazen foot. Sure enough, water spurted out, caught the sunlight, made us giggle with delight. All four of us were soon running around under the canopy of our makeshift sprinkler.

In my memory, the activity lasted all afternoon; in reality, it was probably only a half hour. "It is easy to believe in such moments that water was made primarily for blessing," writes Marilynne Robinson, "and only secondarily for growing vegetables or doing the wash."[6] None of us wanted the afternoon to end, and the videotaped footage of our timid tapping and our spontaneous shrieks still brings back the feeling of an experience we were never able to replicate. We all seemed to know that the nozzle's sticking in such a way was an anomaly—that each time we tapped it might be the last time it would work. Perhaps that is what made the day so enchanting.

I think of that afternoon when I read Jesus' words: "Whoever believes in me, streams of living water will flow from within him." Perhaps it's the joy of the day, so particularly documented in my mind, that brings that correlation. Perhaps it's how the hose seemed to take on a life of its own. *Living* water. Or perhaps it's how the water caught the light, sparkling and crystalline for a few seconds before it splashed down. Whatever the reason, the love of God is an erratic garden hose for me. I imagine it, when pressed, sticking open for an unpredictable period of time, spraying out blessing upon blessing upon blessing on anyone who happens beneath its umbrella. And I remember my baptism.

Pentecost

cultivation

This is the third summer in a row I decided to try gardening. We have this backyard that could look like something out of a storybook with lush plants and flowers springing and curling out from the beds, but I tend to kill approximately two-thirds of the things I put in the ground. It's an expensive and not very fruitful game I play every spring. So this year, I decided to try vegetables instead of flowers and enlisted the help of my earthy friend Shelley. Shelley is the editor of a gardening blog, so I figured she, if anyone, would know why I had unwittingly become the Dr. Kevorkian of the floral world.

I was especially skeptical that my garden would grow this year because we were starting from seeds. When Shelley spilled the contents of the carrot-seed packet in her hands, I almost laughed out loud. Those ridiculous specks of nothing? There was no way this was going to work. Please understand: it's not that I don't believe that seeds grow into plants (I'm not quite that naïve, although I do sometimes think the antibacterial soap industry is in cahoots with the scientists and has completely fabricated germs), but rather that I don't think they'll grow if *I* plant them. I prefer wasting my money on starter plants: seeds that real gardeners, those with more patience or sprinklers on timers, have nurtured into something that actually looks alive. But Shelley insisted.

I, along with most of the nation, was suddenly interested in "going green" and "eating organic." If this was the way I was going to get my own free, organic, "green" vegetables, then I was going to do it. I am a smart person, right? Other people—people who accidentally set their houses on fire on the Fourth of July and people who play the lottery—have done it, right? Why couldn't I?

My impression of the growing process involved me putting the aforementioned speck into the dirt and letting it spark and twist and start getting bigger with a *woomp woomp woomp* sound while I watered it and gave it little pep talks. Perhaps sometimes God would do the watering for me, with His giant watering can in the sky. We would work out a schedule.

I didn't inherit my grandmother's skill in gardening. She fostered a hummingbird's paradise on her little backyard patio in the Escondido hills. Since the weather was mild all year, snapdragons, birds of paradise, and lush ferns flourished even in the fall and winter when her grandchildren would converge on her tiny town house for Thanksgiving dinner or a Christmas gift exchange. I was never very impressed by Grandma's garden as a kid; the patio garden had always been there, a tiny oasis amid the more desertlike brush that naturally covered the sloping hills. I took it for granted. But it is the place I associate most with her, and I remember her tiny, nimble fingers working to prune dead leaves from a ficus tree or refill the bird feeders hanging from the eaves of the house.

She was a slight woman with a hug that could leave bruises. I would brace myself for those bone-crushing embraces, and though we loved her, my siblings and I would try our best to avoid her greetings. We wished she was more of a handshake-type person, but she never was. Even at her most frail, right before her death, her hugs didn't get less vehement.

i've always found it interesting that one can walk into a home improvement store and buy dirt.

"Peep peep peep," she'd trill in her thick Dutch accent. Her birdcall was as much a sound of the garden as the little rock waterfall, but the birds never needed much enticing because Grandma's spirit, unlike her hugs, was gentle and nurturing. I don't think gardening was something she learned; I think it was somehow always part of her nature.

The Saturday morning that Shelley arrived, I was feeling optimistic. I'd purchased a few seed packets, some gardening soil, and a few broccoli starter plants—just so I'd have something to eat when the seeds didn't work. Shelley showed me how to prepare the soil with the hoe so the seeds had more room in the loose dirt to move around and *woomp woomp* without feeling claustrophobic. Shelley said my soil was good: full of earthworms, rich in color, lots of decomposing organic matter, which it turns out, is the upside to not raking for a year. We just needed to get rid of the rocks, and it would be ready for planting.

I've always found it interesting that one can walk into a home improvement store and buy dirt. Really, any kind of dirt: garden soil, sand, dirt with gravel, dirt with fertilizers, dirt with weed killers, a dirt and clay mix. What's even more interesting is how I tend to trust the bagged stuff more than I do the stuff that has been sitting in my flower beds, part of its own little ecosystem, for billions of years. Or at least since the house's previous owners put it in there a decade ago. Despite Shelley's insistence that my soil was healthy, and the fact that the weeds were sure flourishing in it, I was convinced that the $4.99 variety would be the magic bullet that gave me a bountiful harvest.

"Should we add some of this Garden Soil?" I asked, pointing to the green-and-yellow bag. I said it like it was supposed to be capitalized, too. Like the garden soil that was in my garden was very lowercased compared to the Garden Soil in the bag.

"We could," Shelley said. "Or we can just add some of those dead leaves you've got in that pile." *Dead leaves*. As if they would do anything. They were *free* and completely useless! In fact, they were sitting in the pile because I was too lazy to bag them up and set them out with the rest of the garbage where they belonged.

"Okay, we can do both," I said judiciously. But when Shelley examined the bagged soil, she said it had too much clay; the seeds wouldn't thrive. I threw in a little along the edges of the beds anyway. Just in case. I don't know when this overdependence on purchased things began. Maybe in middle school, when I was absolutely sure that LA Gears would make me popular. Since my mom never bought the expensive shoes for me, I settled for an LA Gear key chain I'd gotten from my cousin, which I attached to the zipper of my backpack.

At least people would know I supported the wearing of the LA Gears even if I didn't have them on my feet. Maybe it started even before that, but however it began, I'm now firmly entrenched in my status as Consumer, perhaps even stuck.

I knew there was a problem when I discovered that wandering the aisles of my local Target store helped cure my bouts of loneliness and sadness. I didn't even need to buy anything; just knowing the racks of candlesticks, bed linens, trash bags, and gardening tools were there comforted me. I'd spend hours perusing the end-of-aisle clearance items, maybe taking a brief break at the patio furniture display with a bag of trail mix that I'd pay for in a moment. It got even worse when I spoke about it to friends and they said they did the same thing. Retail therapy indeed. We are a nation of people who find solace in things, but not just any things: the things we manufacture. A certain kind of pride has welled up in our collective bosom: if there is a problem, an irritant, or a gap, we can invent and patent a product that will fix it, soothe it, or fill it. No wonder they air infomercials in the middle of the night; the sleepless worriers can watch a problem defined and solved in half an hour. The magic product doesn't solve everything, of course, maybe just the scuff marks on the kitchen linoleum, but it does solve something—for only four easy payments of $19.95 plus shipping. And so Garden Soil is better than garden soil, the premade holes in Abercrombie's jeans are more fashionable, somehow, than holes that

i knew there was a problem when i discovered that wandering the aisles of my local Target store helped cure my bouts of loneliness and sadness.

come naturally with years of wear, and a scheduled C-section will deliver a baby more conveniently than pushing. We often trust our products and our inventions more than we trust ourselves, more than we trust nature, more than we trust God. What we end up with is usually just a temporary fix or worse, a subpar version of what we really crave.

Things and *stuff* are two words that most writing teachers will implore you never to use. Those words aren't concrete enough to give readers a mental picture, they say. Be specific! they say. But though the terms are abstractions in writing, stuff and things are more concrete in real life than we give them credit for. I sit now surrounded by stuff: my leather purse, a cell phone, a water glass, the baby's high chair, a blue cotton sweater, the television remote, a pile of bills, a bottle of aspirin. Things are everywhere, and I am constantly yielding to their power. Before I get up from this writing desk, for instance, I will instinctually check the time and the voice mail on my phone. I'll put on a sweater to cure the slight chill in the office, take a sip of water to satisfy my thirst, an aspirin for that headache that just won't subside. I will have to move the high chair in order to get out of my office, and I will be forced to carry my purse if I decide to leave the house. And the bills. Of course, the bills.

advertisements work because they sell us on a quality of life that we are somehow dumb enough or desperate enough to believe we could attain through a product.

I don't tend to ask for many physical things in prayer. Somehow, no matter how much I like the new Prius and think that my driving it would be better for the planet and for me, I can't bring myself to ask God to send me a Prius. A blue one. With one of those giant bows and heated seats. Instead, I ask for things like patience or security or certainty. Those words smack of the kind of requests I imagine God is eager to answer. I think, though, that I never give Him time to. The amount of patience I possess is only slightly higher than the amount of faith, so instead of waiting, I hurry off to buy yoga videos and thirty-minute-meal cookbooks. These will help with the patience issues, I tell myself. I buy life, dental, health, car, house, fire, and earthquake insurance to give me security. I look to lots of books for certainty and for answers. Some would argue that those products are, in some way, God's answer to my prayers. But I tend to think I've gotten very comfortable shelving God totally in favor of some magical new product.

Advertisements and marketing plans don't work because they sell us stuff. They work because they sell us on a quality of life that we are somehow dumb enough or desperate enough to believe we could attain through a product. I have actually gotten my credit card out of my wallet a few times while watching the infomercial for the Jack LaLanne juicer, and not because his soy spinach milk shake looks so delicious. It's because he's selling health, and I want that.

I don't think that the Christian response is to forgo the doctor's office in favor of praying away appendicitis, nor do I think that aspirin is the wrong choice for a headache. I think car insurance is a good idea and a legal necessity, and I think that I'm very lucky to live in a place where all of those things exist. But I do believe that I need to work especially hard not to settle for the tangible, immediate results that stuff can give me.

A Jeep commercial on television declares: "The things we make, make us." It shows Americans in all sorts of occupations "making" everything from the front bumper of a Jeep to long lines of electrical conductors. It argues that our identities are inextricably intertwined with our things. The very idea firmly imprisons man in what he's manufactured. We've said similar things before, but to a different end; the mantra "Don't let the things you own own you" spoke against the materialism that so easily creeps in to take over our lives. Funny that, though we don't want things to own us, we don't mind giving them the power to define us. The problem is no longer that we merely love our stuff, but that we find our meaning in it, our being, our life-blood. The things we make become the evidence of what we value, what we know, and just how much potential we possess.

we don't need a pillar of smoke to guide us through the desert because someone probably has GPS.

It's not surprising, then, that we tend to trust what is measurable and concrete. That's why Professor David Jauss observes that even his writing students "don't trust writers to know, much less tell, the truth about their own art. However, they do tend to trust scientists." A poet is allowed to have his own opinion, but you can't argue with a scientist's. A scientist's opinion is reiterated by research and findings, by evidence, and by the weightiest thing of all: proof. Excepting their somewhat questionable findings on germs, it seems that those guys are getting results. But the truths of the soul can't be measured with quite the same precision that the spread of smallpox can, so the humanities seem less trustworthy in our culture, less sure, more open for debate and interpretation.

Our things—the concrete evidence of what we value—are part of what has conditioned us to believe that Specificity and Tangibility reign. The craving for specifics can often usurp faith, which has not been a valuable commodity in America for some time. The craving for the tangible posits a problem for Christians, whose very identities rest in the fact that we believe in that which we "cannot see." New products, coming out at warp speed, teach us to trust in what is newest, what is next, what is yet to be invented or discovered. We are taught that "God helps those who help themselves" (many American Christians even believe that Ben Franklin's aphorism is found in the Bible), so we look for ways to avoid waiting on God. We don't need a pillar of smoke to guide us through the desert because someone probably has GPS. We don't need manna to fall daily from heaven because I've got dinners for the next two weeks stocked up in my downstairs freezer and four coupons to Chick-fil-A. We don't need that choir of angels; they would be drowned out by our iPods, anyway. I, for one, would be a terrible Old Testament Israelite.

In the weeks after Shelley had helped me plant my garden, I'd wander into the backyard with my watering can, anxiously leaning in, checking the soil for new growth. I still couldn't tell the difference between a weed and the beginnings of a vegetable, so I'd celebrate whenever anything poked its leafy head from under the dirt. The green beans took off within a matter of days, stunning me so much that I ran inside to get Scott, dragged him outside so he could witness for himself the wonder of the birth of organic matter. He didn't seem as enthusiastic as I was, but then, he never had the same doubts about the viability of seeds that I did. While the beans flourished almost immediately, the broccoli plants didn't fare quite as well. They were ravaged by calculating squirrels with handlebar mustaches or maniacal rabbits who insist upon speaking in the third person or whatever other hateful creatures you can conjure up in the depths of your imagination. All that was left was a shallow hole where the plant used to be. I began to sympathize with the Gardener in the Peter Cottontail stories. Flopsy and Mopsy could bite me, as far as I was concerned, and the next day I put up a little fence and researched the most potent chemicals to keep them from stealing the rest of my food.

After the initial thrill of discovering the feathery carrot tops, nothing much seemed to happen. They sat there, in a line, being puny. Some of the other plants got bigger slowly. Especially the tomato plants, which soon needed stakes to help them stand upright. But nothing grew big enough to eat, and there were very few little green beginnings of tomatoes, mostly just leaves. I continued buying my produce in the grocery stores, continued dreaming about that day when I wouldn't need to.

My friend Jess, who had planted her garden at around the same time, came to church one day in late June bragging about the overflow of tomatoes she had. She even brought me a few in a little paper bag. Her family of four couldn't eat them fast enough, apparently. So I ate her stupid, delicious tomatoes. My pep talks in the garden gradually deteriorated into rants, and I realized that I was becoming the verbally abusive coach who tried to intimidate her players into winning. Unfortunately, my carrots didn't fall for this tough-guy routine.

My thoughts eventually turned back to Garden Soil, and how there must be some sort of Plant Fertilizer that would remedy this puny plant situation. A trip to the hardware store confirmed my suspicions: right next to all the dirt was all the crap, and it ranged so terrifically in price that I couldn't decide which variety to buy. Naturally, I assumed that the most expensive one would yield the best results. ("You get what you pay for," I overheard another customer say as she loaded her cart with the newest, most nutritionally enhanced variety of dung.) But I was still a poor graduate student who was growing vegetables for the sole purpose of not wanting to pay for them, so I left the store with something midline in price and productivity.

I don't remember if my grandmother used this sort of gardening aid or not. I never asked her things like that. In fact, I asked her fairly few questions at all in my growing-up years. I endured her tight embrace and gave her the obligatory hug when I saw her, let her smack me violently on the side of my face with her lipsticked kiss, and then went off to make trouble with my young cousins.

Only later, after I was grown and married and Grandma was showing early signs of dementia, did I began to realize how much I didn't know about her. There were snippets, of course, about how she, a nurse in a mental hospital, met Grandpa during World War II when he was hiding out from the German army. The stories reminded me of Ernest Hemingway plotlines and of *The Diary of Anne Frank*. They seemed so far removed from my grandparents that I didn't bother writing anything down, or even keeping the details in my memory for long. When Grandma's memory started deteriorating, though, I was seized with a feeling of urgency. She and I were at my parents' house for dinner one night, and we ended up washing dishes together. She told me stories of her youth—stories that were so embedded in her mind that they came out clear and intelligible. Even when she couldn't remember who I was, she could remember details of the years leading up to World War II with clarity.

"I had a jacket with fur on the collar. It was very good-looking. Sexy," she told me with a giggle. "I'd ride on the back of Jack's motorcycle. We went all over Holland like this."

I tried to imagine it. I couldn't. But she went on anyway, not particularly caring if I was caught up or not, or if I could understand her through her accent, describing what it was like when Grandpa had to take apart his little scooter and bury it to save it from being confiscated by German soldiers. She talked about the war ending, about when she and Grandpa married and moved to Canada, where she'd eventually give birth to my mom. She talked about her life as a missionary and her struggles to learn English when they finally moved to California with their family of seven. Those later stories were easier for me to grasp, the stories of her as a mother and care-giver. I didn't know her as a young woman in love, a wearer of fur-collared jackets or nurse's uniforms, an adventure seeker who didn't mind starting over again in places all over the world. And so, over dirty dishes, I learned about her life.

When Grandma died, I flew back home for her funeral. The church was full, and many of those in attendance were people I'd never met. Some of them were very old, like Grandma, and the memories they shared stretched back over decades. The stories sounded familiar this time around, and old men and women filled in gaps in my incomplete and often inaccurate understanding of my grandmother's life. In the stretch of an hour and a half, I felt something akin to what the men and women of the early Church must have in the upper room during Pentecost. That little gathering, which has since come to be regarded as the first official "meeting" of the Church, occurred after a particularly important person's death. There was no fire from heaven at our meeting, but we told stories, remembered, and enjoyed each other's company. We spoke of the ways God worked through one woman's life and wondered how many people she had touched with her love and compassion. Then we ate.

The Church, even before it was the Church, existed and flourished because people told stories. The entire Old Testament is, well, a testament to this idea. The stories of Abraham, Moses, Esther, and Jeremiah were kept alive because people told and retold them. We do the same things now on Sunday mornings in little A-frame churches, weeknights in bars over margaritas, and sometimes while washing dishes. This centuries-old game of Telephone might mean, empirically, that the facts don't always line up perfectly, as hundreds of skeptics have pointed out. But facts are not usually the purpose of stories. Unless, of course, you are a crime-scene investigator. Instead, the Bible is a collection of stories that help us remember God's faithfulness to all generations. To trust what is age-old is a different thing altogether from trusting what is next.

But later in Acts comes a verse that people don't often bring up in sermons or conversation: "All the believers were together and had everything in common. Selling their possessions and goods, they gave to anyone as he had need." It's interesting that the story of Pentecost is followed by this line. The telling of stories and living together seem at odds with the accumulation of things. Indeed, this has made me question how much togetherness we might sacrifice, intentionally or not, because of our stuff. I wonder this when most of the college students I pass on campus are wearing earbuds and lost in their own, individualized concerts that nobody else is privy to. Or when I'm stuck in traffic on the freeway, the carpool lane is empty, and I'm aware that each of these little metal pods, the ones jockeying for the least congested lane, is occupied, usually, by a single person. Or when I hear of friends who, when expanding their families, also feel the need to expand their houses so that each warm body can have a room all his or her own. I think about people who lived in centuries past, women who'd go in groups to the town's well to gather water, or families crammed into one small living space, or tribes and clans who hunted, ate, and lived in the same space. They did this mostly out of necessity: the way you

to trust what is age-old is a different thing altogether from trusting what is next.

lived depended on the help and company of other people. Now that one can do virtually everything he or she needs to do from home, by one's self, without any human contact, some of us choose to live like this. And even if we aren't quite so extreme to live as hermits, we often make small choices that give us our own space, or at least a bit of distance from our fellow humans. We like this choice, which is one of the reasons we like our stuff, and why more and more often, the products we create have identifying words like *individual, personal,* and *customized.*

The evening following my grandmother's funeral, the family went over to my aunt's house where Grandma had been living the last months of her life. On two folding tables in the garage, my aunt had set out the last of Grandma's possessions, which, to be honest, were very unimpressive: some costume jewelry, a few mismatched teacups, an oil painting or two, a variety of needlepoints and old photo albums, some knickknacks I remembered from the town house, but little else. Our inheritance.

"I think you should take this," my aunt said. She was holding a necklace pendant that was simple and small: just a circular painting of a windmill done in Delft blue, the silver casing black and tarnished on one side. It wasn't even on a chain. It was perfect.

We all left with trinkets like that: my cousin loved the strand of fake pearls she'd inherited, and my sister the champagne glasses that Grandma probably picked up at a big-box store. My mom's first request was for the button box, which, just like it sounds, is nothing more than a box my grandmother had used to store the extra buttons that came with fancy sweaters and travel sewing kits. They were the mismatched nomads of the sewing world, and Mom remembers playing with the collection as a girl. So do I. No expensive silverware for us, no gold lockets or antique nightstands. In fact, I will never brag about a thing my grandma "passed down," though I often admire the valuable heirlooms my friends have inherited from their relatives.

"She was always like that," Mom told me when I commented on the lack of Grandma's stuff in the garage. "Since she and Dad were on the move so often, she'd just sell everything. She didn't hold too tightly to her things."

It was lucky, I thought, that I got to know her even a little bit before she was gone. I thought about people who aren't so lucky, people who attempt to hold on to the memories of people they never really knew by collecting the stuff they left behind. I've listened to news stories about how families of the very rich sometimes engage in long legal battles over possessions not designated clearly enough in the will. I try to believe the best in these people, that they aren't fighting over valuable things simply because they're valuable; rather, the stuff becomes a way to remember the departed. A limited-edition Aston Martin with custom seats and paint is not the rightly shaped peg to fill the hole, but it's something. Likewise, there are many religious people who feel desperate for some *thing* to prove their faith—an artifact, a relic, a sign. I don't blame them, certainly, and I often crave that, too. But just as the Shroud of Turin or a chunk of wood someone claims was part of his cross can do little to help me understand Jesus, the items on the folding tables in my aunt's garage were nothing more than old stuff, leftovers from a life more focused on love than on acquisition.

I never got much from my garden this year. One serrano pepper and a mushy green bell pepper that grew no larger than an egg. I thought for a while that better Soil or expensive Fertilizer would have done the trick. Shelley tells me the plants probably just needed regular attention from me, and maybe a little more sunlight.

Ordinary Time

the preacher's wife

ꕥ

Now may I speak kindly but firmly to you few who
may not care how you look? You are not being spiritual. You are hurting your testimony and shaming not
only your church people but probably your husband.
May I remind you that your husband is constantly with
well-dressed women? A mental image of you, slouching
around home in a robe and slippers is not very good
protection against those few women every minister
must contend with who deliberately try to attract him,
and the occasional one who tries to break up his home
or entice him into a secret love affair. Ask God to
give you a real interest in looking right.

—DOROTHY PENTECOST[1]

Being a pastor's wife comes with a lot of responsibility. At least
that's what I've heard from my mother-in-law, Vonnie. And
her mother, too. Both pastors' wives, they had to grapple with
different generational assumptions concerning what a pastor's
wife should be or do, and a few of the stereotypes have stuck

around. A pastor's wife should respond appropriately to all announcements, public and private, from the parishioners. She should appear concerned when someone falls ill, pleased when someone "comes to the Lord," and serene and worry-free even in the face of hardship. She should wear skirts and nylons and enough makeup to look respectable but not too pretty. She should sing or play the piano—extra points for doing both. A pastor's wife should volunteer in the nursery on some Sundays and be generally aware of what's going on with children's ministry most of, if not all, the time. She should know how to cook a roast and be ready to entertain guests in her home at a moment's notice. She should sit in the front row at church. I find it all somewhat reminiscent of old-world England, and might sum it up in a quote from Lady Grantham of *Downton Abbey:* "The truth is neither here nor there. It's the look of the thing that matters."

My mother-in-law fits the bill for a pastor's wife in a lot of ways. She's beautiful, stylishly dressed, appropriately concerned about people, kind, generous, gifted with a killer singing voice, and a wonderful cook. She has told me that church life has forced her to become more of an extrovert than she naturally is, but this is a small compromise for anyone to make, and perhaps even a beneficial one. I suppose this ability to maintain selfhood even in the presence of rather strict presuppositions must have come from her parents.

Bus and Dixie, as they were always known, were not overly concerned with maintaining the rather stodgy, Dimmesdale-esque facade of a pastoral family when Bus was in the pulpit. This is not to say that they didn't hold *any* of the views common to their generation—Vonnie remembers being told on many occasions that she couldn't participate in something or act a certain way because she was the pastor's daughter—but, it seems to me at least, that they bucked the trend most of the time. As the story goes, one night when Bus and Dixie were entertaining the District Bigwig and his wife for dinner, Vonnie's twin brothers thought it would be funny to convince then-six-year-old Vonnie to gallop into the front room with a men's protective cup around her head like a hat. "I'm a jockey! I'm a jockey!" she shouted, much to the chagrin of the church leaders. I don't know exactly how Mrs. Bigwig had responded to such a show from the pastor's daughter, but Bus and Dixie laughed about it then and continued to tell the story long after Vonnie had grown up, so they hadn't seen the incident as much of a stain on their reputations.

Much more stringent guidelines for what a pastor's wife should look like come from what I've read in books. While staying with Scott's parents one time, I found a book on the guest room bookshelf titled *The Pastor's Wife and the Church* by Dorothy Pentecost. Next to it were *Rejoice: You're a Minister's Wife* and *Especially for Ministers' Wives: 125 Practical Ideas on Parsonage Management, Interior Decorating, Entertaining, Showers, Family Worship, Budgeting, Gift Ideas, Outreach Projects, and Meditations*. Even a brief skimming of these tomes exhausted me. One chapter outlined how a pastor's wife should dress: "She should appear as attractively dressed as possible all the time. She represents not only her husband but the church and the Lord. Many times the way she looks may have a great effect on the Lord's work."[2] Hmm.

While I never realized the extent to which my appearance might hinder the Lord's work, Pentecost goes on to detail the appropriate length of a pastor's wife's skirt hem, why it's important to leave your bedroom in the morning completely dressed for the day, and how to "judge your style and type of dressing according to the average woman in the church. Do not set your standards by the way the wealthy dress, or feel that you must dress like the poorest."[3] (Since reading this, by the way, I've been prone to assessing the dress of the women in my church during the sermons and lumping them into three categories: (1) Wealthy, Overblown Richie-Richersons; (2) Poor, Sad Walmart Wilmas; and (3) Totally Average and Non-Noteworthy Netties. Which, I'm sure you'll agree, is absolutely biblical.)

presidents' wives must know this feeling, and the wives of rock stars who are prone to biting off the heads of various kinds of poultry during shows; so i feel a certain affinity for those women.

There were instructions on weight management, blurbs about kitchen curtains and bathroom accessories, and a complete chapter called "Are Your Attitudes Showing?" To be fair, all three of these books were published in the late 1960s and early '70s, so we have to judge them as products of these time periods and take into account that a lot of drugs were being done and perhaps had gotten into the air and somehow thwarted the common sense of nearly everyone who was living. (When Vonnie saw me reading the Pentecost book, she asked, with panic in her eyes, whether or not she'd underlined anything. She visibly relaxed when I shook my head. "Oh, good.")

Although things have changed slowly, and the spouses of pastors are not held to quite the same standards as they once were, I often hear apologies from friends for an off-color joke or bad word when they discover I'm married to a pastor. These moments of backpedaling are probably not as numerous as what Scott hears when he discloses that he *is* a pastor, but still, one friend recently wrote on Facebook, "I can't believe I just wrote that on my pastor's wife's wall!" And all she was writing about were a certain group of nice-looking vampires. It's a strange thing to be categorized so swiftly and then judged as such when the role is solely dependent on what your husband does for a living. Presidents' wives must know this feeling, and the wives of rock stars who are prone to biting off the heads of various kinds of poultry during shows; so I feel a certain affinity for those women. You tend to be treated as an extension of his role: a prop or another line on his résumé. One woman I know was asked to be present at her husband's interview at a new church. The church board wanted to check her out—and they wanted her to know that they were hiring *her,* too. After hearing this, she and her husband knew that they'd find a different church home and declined even the interview.

There are few women who are routinely labeled by their husband's profession; you don't hear people referred to as "the accountant's wife" or "the butcher's wife" anymore, thank goodness. I suppose this went out of fashion around the same time mail stopped being addressed to The Reverend Mrs. Scott Savage. I'm not sure if this is an issue for the men who happen to be pastors' husbands or not. The term *pastor's husband* sounds as foreign as *First Gentleman,* and, though there's bound to be a woman president sometime in the near future, I don't see that particular label ever catching on. Regardless, the line between being a pastor's wife and having a husband who happens to be a pastor, while distinct for me, isn't very clear for some people.

Scott and I met in college at a small, Nazarene school in Southern California. Most of the girls there were mildly obsessed with finding a husband, so much so that jokes about getting a "ring by spring" and obtaining one's MRS Degree ran rampant throughout the girls' dorms. (After spending four years at a much larger, much secular-er university for graduate studies, I've found that this is a particular quirk of small, Christian schools and does not, indeed, happen everywhere. Whew.) For reasons that totally elude me, many of these girls also dreamed of marrying a pastor, and thus the religion majors got way more game than they probably deserved. Though I've made some ridiculous mistakes in the past—driving away with the gas hose still attached to my car, tossing my non-Christian music collection because I thought it would bring me closer to God, Birkenstocks with socks—this fixation was not among them. I was not at all interested in finding a husband, and even less interested in finding a pastor husband. I *did,* however, think it would be pretty cool to find a boyfriend.

I got married relatively young by today's standards (I was twenty-three), but I still remember years of being dateless. I grew up pretty confident that I could ace a spelling test, but not at all convinced that my nose fit correctly on my face. It was the nostrils that could flare to the size of a storybook dragon's that really got to me. Nostril flaring could have been a pretty good party trick, actually, had I not been so utterly ashamed of them that I practiced contracting my face muscles and sucking in enough air that they'd appear smaller to the casual observer. I knew that I wasn't ugly, in the duckling sense of the word, but I also knew that I wasn't the kind of girl that boys generally sought out. Girls with small breasts, an introverted demeanor, and high moral standards don't tend to hear the phone ring off its hook in high school.

So the goal of Finding a Boyfriend was at the top of my prayer request list. Right above, you know, less important things like food for the poor and sight for the blind. I agonized over it. Why didn't boys like me? Was it my dragon nostrils? Would I ever, my sixteen-year-old self wondered, get *married*?

My methodology for dating was simple. I'd target one boy—usually one wildly inappropriate for me—and find every picture of him in the yearbook. I'd figure out what my initials would be if I did, in fact, marry him. I blushed whenever his name came up in casual conversation. I'd look for him across the commons area, just so I'd know where he was in case of a fire or a flood (this is why it was better if he was tall). I'd try to figure out his class schedule. Then I'd wait for him to reciprocate. He (and, offhand, I can think of at least seven boys' names that could replace that pronoun) never did. Shocking.

Other boys tried to. Nice boys. Boys my mother loved and who won superlative awards like Kindest Eyes and Most Likely to Win the

girls with small breasts, an introverted demeanor, and high moral standards don't tend to hear the phone ring off its hook in high school.

Nobel Peace Prize. Boys who wrote love letters on stationery they borrowed from their mothers and that chronicled all the things they liked about me using complete sentences, correct punctuation, and absolutely no variations of the word *sexy*. The kind of guys I envision my daughter dating. But I knew what I wanted—which, remember, was wildly inappropriate for me—and I'd wait for that.

By the time I hit college, I felt like something of an anomaly in the dating world. Maybe every young adult in America feels this way. But the representation of what it meant to be young and collegiate was a far cry from the life I was living. I couldn't recognize myself in the sexualized, carefree stereotypes I saw around me. I had only just had my first kiss a few months before. It had happened on a historic hotel rooftop, the evening lit up by thousands of Christmas lights. He was one of only two guys I had dated throughout high school, and that was because he was a singer in a Christian band. And rather cute. Perfect, except that when he leaned in, I jumped back like a startled squirrel and totally embarrassed both him and myself. Our relationship lasted all of a month, and that longevity was probably owed to the fact that we lived in different towns. I spent a month swooning over him during shows and apologizing for him whenever he spoke. It was not a good match. And though I blame it partly on him for being the kind of person who routinely added sugar to his water at restaurants, I know I was too judgmental and vain to really deserve him anyway. After that brief stint, I was more careful about dating anyone I was not crazy about, and thus went on even fewer dates with even fewer boys.

When I met Scott in the fall of our freshman year in college, he was dating someone else. He was always dating someone else, even though he appeared pretty oblivious to the dozens of girls who followed him around campus with the three-girls-to-every-guy attendance ratio spurring them on. He has always been rather unassuming, and in college Scott was preoccupied with baseball, school, and the upkeep of the rusted orange Volkswagen Bug that was laughably small for his six-foot four-inch frame. I wrote him off as way out of my league and continued stalking the tattooed Bible study leader my friend had introduced me to. She was also rather interested in him, and because that made him wildly inappropriate for me, I was not to be deterred.

It's hard to say what changed in me, but somewhere along the way, I stopped wanting all the boys I knew I'd never have. Or maybe it was simply that the boy I thought I'd never have actually wanted to have me. Regardless, I started pining after Scott sometime during my sophomore year in college. He had broken up with his latest girlfriend, and though he and I knew each other, we were not good friends by a long shot. I fell back on my usual, angsty MO, but a friend of mine decided she'd speed things up a little and just told Scott that I liked him. When I think back, the days of silently assessing whether or not Scott was in the cafeteria were long and emotionally arduous. In reality, however, we were holding hands by New Year's Day. Our first date was at the Tournament of Roses Parade, where we set up sleeping bags in the gutter in Pasadena across from a discount Oriental rug shop and a Subway restaurant. Very romantic. Scott—if you don't count the sugar-water guy—was my first *real* boyfriend. The kind who wrote me cheesy love songs and played them on his guitar, who surprised me with carnations on our first Valentine's Day together and forgave me for calling them the "weeds of the floral world" before I knew they were waiting for me on my dorm bed, and who I never apologized for in public—wouldn't even know what to apologize for. This is how it was at the beginning, during those months and years of brand-new love.

> *i find myself praying—in the corners of my mind that are a bit harder to control—that god will continue* not *calling me to become a missionary.*

Dorothy Pentecost writes that being the wife of a pastor is a calling. One mustn't marry a minister for love alone, she says, for the local church's demands on the wife—even though it's not technically *her* job—are as great as they might be on her husband. While I understand the logic behind such a belief, I can't say I felt any such calling.

When I was young, I felt called to some things—like marrying a very attractive man, succeeding in a job that involved taste-testing various new flavors of ice cream, buying a moderately big house that had a slide in place of stairs, and giving birth to talented and beautiful children who would help take care of me when I got old and probably rather fat from all that ice cream. I realize now that these dreams may be the religious equivalent of how every short, uncoordinated little boy wants to become an NBA star, but back then it made a lot of sense. If I'm honest, it still sounds good. And if I continue being honest, most of my prayers concerning a calling are rather self-serving. Like how, every once in a while, I find myself praying—in the corners of my mind that are a bit harder to control—that God will continue *not* calling me to become a missionary in a remote region of South America with a disconcerting person-to-toilet ratio. Then I immediately apologize about the selfishness of that prayer, and begin thinking about how, in order to teach me a lesson in humility or love or generosity, God will probably send me to the very region I didn't want to go to in the first place. Then I apologize again, because it's pretty good odds that God heard that part, too.

It's safe to say that God mostly ignores my requests about what I'd prefer being called to and works with me, with an extraordinary amount of grace, on what I'm actually called to. So, while I somehow scored the attractive husband part of my request, He surprised me with the whole preacher's wife thing.

Scott had kicked around the idea of going into the ministry since high school. Although he was majoring in religion, I half expected him to pursue a baseball career, and I think he did, too. Maybe neither of us really knew how serious he was about it until he got a call from a pastor friend who asked him to be the new youth pastor for his little "restart" church in Los Angeles. (In layman's terms, a "restart" church is basically one that is "broke" and "small.") I suppose that the only wife I've ever been is a pastor's wife because, right after our wedding, we moved into the church parsonage. The house was our only form of payment and was right across the parking lot from the sanctuary; but I suppose that's pretty generous in L.A.

All I'd ever heard about being a pastor's wife was true: people expected things of you. I led the singing. I led the morning Bible studies. I helped with the youth group. I dressed up. I answered the door at six o'clock on Sunday mornings when Catalina, the little old lady who did the flowers for service, bellowed for Scott to open the church. I painted the offices and vacuumed the foyer.

But Scott never expected any of it.

If you ever attend a Christian marriage seminar, a certain passage in Ephesians 5 is bound to come up:

"Wives, be subject to your own husbands, as to the Lord. For the husband is the head of the wife, as Christ also is the head of the church, He Himself being the Savior of the body. But as the church is subject to Christ, so also the wives ought to be to their husbands in everything. Husbands, love your wives, just as Christ also loved the church and gave Himself up for her, so that He might sanctify her, having cleansed her by the washing of water with the word, that He might present to Himself the church in all her glory, having no spot or wrinkle or any such thing; but that she would be holy and blameless. So husbands ought also to love their own wives as their own bodies. He who loves his own wife loves himself; for no one ever hated his own flesh, but nourishes and cherishes it, just as Christ also does the church, because we are members of His body. . . . This mystery is great; but I am speaking with reference to Christ and the church."

This passage is the one that Christian literalists often cite for believing that husbands are the "spiritual heads of the household" and is why feminists in many circles are skeptical of the Bible and of Christianity in general. I happen to interpret the passage very differently—as one in which Paul seeks to describe Christ's relationship to the church by using the imagery of the marriage relationship, or at least how it looked in his time. This does not mean that, because some of the characteristics of marriage have changed over the years, we should disregard this passage. It just means that Paul's letter to the church in Ephesus probably isn't the best go-to spot for marriage advice, just as Leviticus is not the go-to spot for what to do if you have a skin infection, or a ham sandwich, or your period.

all i'd ever heard about being a pastor's wife was true: people expected things of you.

But marriage in *our* time serves as fertile ground for understanding Christ, too, I think. After Scott and I left that first little church in L.A., we moved to Kansas City for him to attend seminary, and now he's the associate pastor at a church called Redemption. I am still a hesitant sort of pastor's wife. I am nothing like what Dorothy Pentecost describes, especially when it comes to my attitudes about the position, which do, sometimes, tend to be "showing." Sometimes I cuss. Sometimes (okay, most of the time) I answer the door for the UPS man at three o'clock in the afternoon in my pajamas. Sometimes I fall asleep in the middle of my prayers. Just the other day, I asked a woman at our church if she had any cancer in her family—after praying fervently for her, not even a year ago, in the wake of her sister-in-law's death from the disease. I am far from being the way I wish I was. This is not to say that I don't dress up for church or help with the children's program—but I definitely don't do those things *because* I am the pastor's wife. And Scott, like it's said of the Lord, doesn't ever judge me by outward appearances, but rather by the heart. He tends to turn Lady Grantham's—and Lady Pentecost's—argument on its head, which is just one of the many things I love about him.

this love has weathered some things; it is comfortable and honest and ridiculous and sometimes unfair.

After almost a decade of marriage, I can't say we don't have our disagreements—one of our best fights in recent memory was regarding Scott's travel toothbrush. The details of the argument are a little blurry, but here's the gist: (Oh, and please imagine Scott talking in a voice that sounds like a cross between LL Cool J and a cartoon bullfrog, as that is the voice I usually employ when telling people stories about Scott's and my arguments. You know, just to emphasize the fact that he was probably wrong.) Now, the gist:

KATIE: Why are you using your travel toothbrush?

SCOTT: I like my travel toothbrush.

KATIE: It doesn't make any sense. It's so flimsy. The top of it folds into the bottom of it.

SCOTT: I like my travel toothbrush.

KATIE: But what are you going to use when you actually travel?

SCOTT: I don't know. Why does it matter to you? I like
    my travel toothbrush.

KATIE: Yes. Okay. You're right. It shouldn't matter to
    me. But you should know that I just bought a whole
    bunch of regular toothbrushes from Costco. I have
    enough regular toothbrushes in the pantry to brush
    the teeth of a very hygienic army. So just in case you
    need a new toothbrush . . .

SCOTT: I like my travel toothbrush.

KATIE: Okay. Yes. I'll back off. But it probably isn't
    that good for your teeth.

The argument went on like that for much longer than it
should have, and both of us went to bed angry. I think both
of us even woke up angry. And then, after we'd had a good
twenty-four hours to think about the idiocy of arguing over
a travel toothbrush, we forgave each other and decided that
I was probably right. (No, that last part is a lie. Scott never
really admitted that I was right. But he did start using a regular toothbrush again after the sting of the loss wore off.)

A fight like this is more indicative of the truth of our marriage now than the cheesy love songs or heartfelt carnations,
and this, I've come to believe, is not a bad thing. This love has
weathered some things; it is comfortable and honest and ridiculous and sometimes unfair. We take turns being "the Christ"
part and "the church" part—because it's unfair to expect the
husband to be the Christ figure all the time, and it's insulting to
believe that a wife never should—and sometimes we fail at both.

•   •   •

When we were trying to sell our house, it sat on the market for more than a year without a buyer. We got very good at making the house "show ready." Potential buyers who walked through did not see cabinet doors left open or dusty blinds and fan blades. They did not see the piles of laundry that sit out, some of it sprayed with stain remover and some of it still, unfortunately, absorbing the stains. No one would guess that, only an hour or so beforehand, stacks of paperwork, scads of toys, and various household cleaning products (all now tucked safely in the trunk of the car) littered countertops and area rugs. Those people saw a bowl of lemons and two place settings on the table, freshly vacuumed carpet, and most of the closets half emptied of things they usually held in order to appear roomier. They saw the appearance of life, but not real life.

on being nice

I am not the nicest person I know. I am not, in fact, even among the top-twenty nicest people I know. This realization came as a bit of a shock, as I grew up a "nice Christian girl" in a little Southern California town. The "nice" and the "Christian" always went together, so much so that I began to think of them as one distinct thing. Nicechristian. At church the message of the sermon was often to be nice. Be nice to your parents, to your Brothers and Sisters in Christ, to your actual brothers and sisters, to your neighbor (this was always said in the singular, but understood as being plural), to your enemies. You pretty much had to be nice to everyone. That was an okay goal for me, to be quite honest. I smiled politely at people I liked and those whom I did not. I shook hands with those who were new to the church, told them where the coffee was if they were interested, directed them to some comfortable seats. All of this was done with good intentions. I wanted the people to be comfy and caffeinated during the service. I wanted them to notice how nice Nicechristians are and to want to be that nice themselves someday.

Interestingly enough, most translations of the Bible never

even use the word *nice*. (The NASB and the NLT both do, but neither teaches that nice is something that one should strive to *be*.) Although I'm sure my pastor didn't simply invent the idea that being nice is part of being Christian, the emphasis put upon it during church does seem a bit suspect. Sermons often stemmed from one of the verses having to do with what is commonly referred to as "the Golden Rule." This tenet is one that most people, religious or not, can agree upon, and some form of it is found in over twenty different sacred texts: "Do unto others as you would have them do unto you." So arose the now-ubiquitous idea of the Nicechristian—a person just spiritual enough to open doors for strangers, refrain from cutting other drivers off in traffic (or at least feel some guilt about it when they do), and offer to let someone with only a few things go in front of him or her in the grocery-store line. To translate it loosely: Don't piss anybody off.

The difficult part of living out a theology of niceness (or nicety?) is that the word has lost all meaning. A day in the park can be nice, an expensive cashmere sweater is nice, an expertly executed jump shot is nice, your grandmother's bingo partner might be very nice, funeral services are usually nice, and probably everything about George Clooney is nice. The word has become so void of meaning that a junior high English teacher I know has declared it "dead" and has its laminated gravestone displayed prominently in her classroom to remind students not to use the word in formal writing. She must be right if the same word can be used to describe both George Clooney and your grandmother's bingo partner.

But the word *nice* is not newly slippery. Since its first

recorded use in AD 1300, *nice* has held a variety of different meanings, fourteen of which are listed in and expanded upon in *The Oxford English Dictionary*. The definitions range from "foolish or silly" to "extravagant or showy." They get as obscure and surprising as "lazy," "cowardly," "effeminate," and "slender," and only one definition comes close to the synonym the thesaurus usually substitutes for *nice,* which, I'm sure you could guess, is *kind.*

the difficult part of living out a theology of niceness is that the word has lost all meaning.

In high school I perfected the art of being nice even when I really wasn't. When a boy named Ted, in whom I was not interested, asked me to the Homecoming Dance, I said yes and acted as if I were very excited. (Really, I wanted to go with the pot-smoking boyfriend of one of the head cheerleaders.) Instead of turning Ted down, I complained incessantly to my best friend about how much I did not want to go with Ted but that I felt bad for him and wanted to be nice. Well, Ted found out. This was not, needless to say, one of my Shining Moments of Niceness. I smoothed things over with Ted, told him I was sorry and that I didn't mean it (as this was the nice way to handle the situation). We ended up going to the dance together, but I think Ted subconsciously got his revenge when he decided to take me to Tony Roma's for dinner and I had to eat barbecue ribs while wearing a formal.

Implemented in this underhanded way, being nice is a way of pretending one is feeling something one is not. It is the heavy frosting you would put over a particularly lumpy cake to make it worthy of presentation. You can manipulate frosting to be as smooth or as textured as desired, you can cover up burned edges, you can even fill in holes made from chunks that stuck to the bottom of the pan. You may have to slather the stuff on with a paddle, but eventually the form of a beautiful cake begins to develop. Frosting, like niceness, disguises unevenness.

I still find that being nice is the easiest pattern of behavior to fall into, especially with people I've either not yet gotten to know or those I have decided I do not like. But my act is getting more impatient and less convincing all the time. Take my interactions with an actual neighbor of mine, Crazy Sandy. Crazy Sandy lived to the right of me and spent most of her time on her porch, looking out over her front yard, which was deco-

frosting, like niceness, disguises unevenness.

rated with egregious amounts of wicker and AstroTurf and an unreasonable number of bird feeders and wind chimes. She must have imagined herself as Snow White as she sprinkled birdseed in front of the gnarly, half-dead tree and filled plastic Cool Whip containers with fresh water for thirsty passersby. The birds and squir-

rels the birdseed attracted hovered around like furry vultures waiting for the next drop. The neighborhood strays stopped by for a drink. Crazy Sandy thought the birds, squirrels, and Humane Society candidates were adorable most of the time, but when she was in a foul mood, I often heard her swearing at an unlucky feline or hapless bird for "crapping on her porch" or some other such animalistic offense. She usually fell into states like these when she thought she was alone, but the giant hedge that grew between her porch and mine sometimes left her thinking she was alone when she actually was not.

When Scott and I moved into our home, Sandy (who had not yet acquired the "Crazy" part of her moniker) welcomed us to the neighborhood by telling us that she had been praying for nice neighbors. She also took the opportunity to identify the people in the neighborhood she considered unsavory: the drug dealers down the block, the boys she suspected of gang-related activity who lived with their grandmother, and the gossipy woman who, for decades, has inhabited the house across the street from hers. Sandy seemed to think the quiet, oak-lined street we lived on was Southern California's own 8 Mile, which would explain the prominently displayed "No Trespassing" sign she had recently put up. Scott and I smiled politely.

I was glad to see that Sandy was an animal lover, because our little black-and-white cat, Emilio, was an outdoor cat. If we kept him cooped up in the house too long, he'd start in with a shrill barrage of complaints. Other neighbors in other apartments and houses have not been bothered by Emilio, have indeed liked him, so I thought Sandy would particularly enjoy having a new feline companion. Sure enough, she began to leave cat food out next to the water dish for Emilio to snack on. He would sun himself on the AstroTurf and listen to the hideously clinky song of the wind chimes in the breeze. That was until something changed.

To this day, I'm still not entirely sure what that something was. Probably it was Emilio's penchant and prowess for killing birds. He'd bring the trophy kills home every now and then, leave them on the porch for Scott or me to find and dispose of. We'd make as sure as possible that Sandy didn't see the trophies, but she was the kind of neighbor who informs you that your gutter is starting to pull away from the house or calls the city to complain that one of the streetlights burned out last Tuesday and still nobody has been by to fix it, so it's difficult to get much past her. When she wasn't outside, she was peering out from behind her curtains.

Sandy began giving me subtle hints that my cat was becoming less and less welcome at her house. She'd casually mention the death of yet another bird, wagging her head back and forth as if to accuse me of aiding and abetting a known murderer, or tell me that someone (she'd yet to discover whom) was scratching at her tree's fragile bark. One day she left a leaflet from the Humane Society titled "Why Keeping Cats Indoors Is More Than Just for the Birds" rubber-banded to my doorknob.

And still she put out cat food.

There is such a thing as being too nice. A man I used to attend church with smiled so much that I cannot remember seeing his face relaxed. It was the sort of smile that dominates a face, dwarfing all the other features behind lips and teeth and gums. He would come over to say hello, his whole self following his smile the way a toddler's body trails after its belly when the child is first learning to walk. I often wondered if he ever took advantage of—or even knew about—the other expressions that his face muscles could muster. Perhaps he really was so nice or so happy that smiles had to ooze out, but interactions with him always left me feeling like a grumpy old hag because

I was not doing "Great!" today; I was usually doing "all right" and even that was a stretch. The fact that he played the bongo drums for the band somehow made everything worse. All of that bouncing.

My closest friends smile, but only when it is absolutely necessary. They have biting senses of humor, they take prescription drugs for attitude adjustments, they never use the word *blessed* in conversation. I love them because of these reasons, not in spite of them. It is like my friend Emily says about crocheting pot holders—sometimes the imperfections are so important that she goes out of her way to put them in. They prove that the pot holder spent time in someone's hands, that it wasn't manufactured in some impersonal assembly line.

"You know, Emilio spends an awful lot of time in my yard," Crazy Sandy said to me one day as I was unloading groceries. "I wonder why he doesn't like to be at your house."

I struggled with the paper sack and gallon of milk.

"You might try making your porch a little more comfortable for him," she went on. "Try putting some food out or a blanket."

"Okay," I said. I was getting tired of the little asides, and I had, on more than one occasion, unloaded my anger on my husband. "She's like a mother-in-law who never leaves and can't even make good meat loaf," I told him. But I had promised myself that I'd be nice to her. Even though the gossipy woman across the street had given up on her, even though the elderly couple who loved everyone had warned me about her, and even though the potential gang members kept their distance, I was determined to be a good neighbor. I wanted to show her the love of Christ, dammit. I gritted my teeth into a smile. "Thanks for the advice, Sandy."

So I pulled a plastic chair out of the shed from the backyard. I found a purple towel, folded it invitingly, and placed it on the chair in the sun. I got out some old plastic dishes, filled them with food and water. As I stepped back to look at what I'd accomplished, I couldn't help but notice that my porch was beginning to look a lot like Sandy's.

My pastor, Tim, would have some theological differences with the pastors of my youth, I think. Tim believes that treating people with what he terms "polite indifference" is the same way that people in Jesus' day treated the lepers. In other words, being nice is a way of maintaining social decorum without ever really seeing people. This shot my whole plan with Sandy in the proverbial foot. I was not surprised to hear about it in church, though, as I was doing my best to avoid God on the subject, and it has been my experience that God never stays avoided for very long. I knew that the bubbling anger I experienced whenever Sandy would come over to tell me that our dogs sure barked a lot when we were away or that my friend's car was parked too close to her lawn was spiritually unhealthy, but it had become an obsession to be nice to her no matter what she said or did. I was Captain Ahab and she was my white whale. My arsenal: friendly smiles, polite waves, and fudge on Christmas.

When I got home from work one day, Sandy was outside talking to Woman with Crazy Wiener Dogs from down the street.

Both wore grim expressions. After exchanging pleasantries with me, Wiener Dogs told me that so-and-so had suffered a stroke. Although I didn't recognize the name, I knitted my brows and sighed, asked if so-and-so would be okay.

"They'll probably take her off the life support tonight," Sandy said. She stared at me. "She was the woman who lived at the corner."

And just like that, the shallowness of my relationship with Sandy, with all of my neighbors, was exposed. I knew I wouldn't notice any difference in the corner house after the woman who used to occupy it was taken off life support. The yard would still be mowed by a husband who was still grieving, the dogs would still be let out to bark feebly at me and mine when we passed by, the Christmas wreath would still be up months after the holiday had passed. I *hadn't* seen my neighbors; I was too preoccupied with being nice.

I couldn't be nice to Sandy anymore after that. For a long time, before she moved away, I wasn't exactly sure what to be. We rarely talked. It took some honest words, some slamming doors, some awkward silences, some angry voices, some tears. And one day, Sandy walked over the invisible line between our yards to show me the frog figurine she had picked up at the thrift store. He was big-eyed, very green, and kneeling in prayer. "The world's gotten so bad that even the animals are praying," she said. I laughed because I knew it was her attempt to be neighborly and kind, not because the joke was funny. Positive interac-

i was doing my best to avoid god on the subject, and it has been my experience that god never stays avoided for very long.

tions with Sandy were always fewer than the awful ones; I always told Scott if I had a "moment" with Sandy, and he did likewise. It was encouraging to hear these because being her neighbor was never easy, but at least the animals were praying.

I often have to remind myself that things of substance do not come easily—and niceness comes easily. We are nice in those brief interactions with drive-thru tellers and clerks at the department store—as we should be—but we all seem to realize that niceness in this sense is only a facade, a way to avoid rudeness and unpleasant encounters. I admit that sometimes I like the facade. But there's no sacrifice in niceness, no difficulty, no striving. Niceness is manufactured, neat and perfect, predictable and uniform. Not as similar to kindness as the thesaurus would have you think. Kindness is so human that it's been mangled up by human hands, twisted into knots by those who aren't sure how to handle it yet, uneven but real.

an evangelism tool

They said they wanted us to feel some solidarity with Christians who were persecuted in places like China and Iraq, so they devised a little game. We were given a head start, like in hide-and-seek, and were to scatter ourselves in the brush along the bleak desert hillside. Our pursuers wore black masks and camo gear. We wore T-shirts from camp two years ago and WWJD bracelets. If we were captured, they said, we'd get a taste of what Christians all over the world had to deal with on a daily basis. *A daily basis.*

So my friend Cana and I ran up the stark slope, our tennis shoes slipping on the grit. We tried to find safe harbor behind a rock or a sage bush, but there wasn't much for hiding behind, and we both knew we'd be among the first to get caught. We giggled too much, which is not a helpful habit for those being pursued by infidels. In our defense, we wouldn't have been quite so tickled had the game been less ridiculous.

Neither of us was in a lighthearted, giggly sort of mood, especially since we hadn't had showers that morning. A water and power outage occurred late the previous evening, leaving us grumpy and somewhat stinky. Shower outages were no laughing matter for Cana and me. We needed to wash and blow-dry our hair the same way others needed food for sustenance. No, the giggling was more a defense mechanism than a reflection of our happiness. Like the "fight or flight" response that animals choose between, we had only two responses when cornered: giggle or cry.

I have virtually no memory of awaiting capture, so it must have happened quickly: two or three masked men bound our wrists, threw pillowcases over our heads, and led us to a small room. I could still see relatively well from under the thin cotton, and I recognized the room as the same one in which we'd sung "Shine, Jesus, Shine" earlier in the day. The blacked-out windows were supposed to make it more ominous, I suppose, or presumably prevent Jesus from shining quite so much. I felt my captor's hot breath on my mask as he led me to a place to sit, cross-legged, on the linoleum. They separated us, like any good terrorists would, and yelled "Denounce Christ!" in threatening voices. This was horrifying, yet strangely funny. I battled within myself for the appropriate response—which was probably to stand up boldly for my faith—but the teenaged girl in me won out. I giggled nervously, which enraged my captors and sent them verbally searching for the worst threats they could imagine. The threats didn't help the giggling, though. The boys playing the role of "captor" were obviously untrained, and the threats were neither creative nor descriptive. It was like your mother warning you you'd better get in bed *or else*. I needed specifics if I was going to buy this whole persecution thing.

The game ended when all of the Christians were captured, so I just waited, making every attempt to contain my laughter, until the room was more populated. And this was how we began training for our mission trip to Sydney, Australia, where we were sure to encounter bands of Christian-hating men armed with floral pillowcases.

it was like your mother warning you you'd better get in bed or else. i needed specifics if i was going to buy this whole persecution thing.

After the persecution exercise, Mike, mastermind behind the whole event, told us we could go back to our bunks and shower: "We turned the water off this morning," he said, "to teach you something." I was not quite sure what that something was, unless it had to do with what a jerk Mike was, but I tried not to give it much thought. Mental diatribes in which one cusses out the leader of one's mission trip are not a healthy means for preparing one's heart for ministry. Besides, I was preoccupied with the worry that he might exchange our cushy plane tickets for passage in the cargo hold of some barge.

I'd been drawn to the trip mostly out of a desire for adventure and for the chance to hang out with friends. It was the summer after my first year in college, so I needed something to do.

"I'm going on a mission trip to Australia," Cana had called my dorm room to tell me. "You should come!"

In my mind, I pictured the Great Barrier Reef and the shirtless, tanned surfers who would be languishing along the shoreline, calling to each other, and maybe to me, in their sexy accents. I would like to minister to them, I thought.

Cana was the singer in a Christian band, one that I had been part of until they realized that my voice was not quite good enough for me to be in any band. It was more suited for singing along to *NSYNC songs in the car, which I did often and quite well. My more talented friends had let me down slowly, and my ego had recovered fairly quickly from the blow. Besides, I was a quiet kid who preferred being near the spotlight, not really in it. I would be quite happy going to Australia with my former bandmates, selling "merch" or leading those whose hearts had been changed during the concerts in brief but vital prayers of salvation. So I enthusiastically paid my deposit and claimed my spot.

The group going to Australia was headed up by a youth organization comprising students from several area churches: Youth for Truth. I'd never met the adult leaders, Mike or his wife Vickie, but I was still under the impression that Christians were generally quite reasonable people. I obviously hadn't yet studied the Crusades, the Spanish Inquisition, or the popularity of Testamints: the breath mints with a Gospel message. We met a week before the trip at a training facility outside of town that was normally used for kids' camps. Until the persecution exercise, everything was bunk beds and campfires, so we were sort of blindsided by the whole business.

Mike and Vickie's son Cory introduced the concept of the Dramas, one of the trip's main forms of "ministering" and something I had not known about prior to training camp. As director, Cory doled out parts to those of us who had never participated.

"Okay," he said, looking in my direction. "You'll be the demon."

"What?"

"The demon. You'll be the demon on Ashley's shoulder who convinces her to go to a party and get drunk."

"But I—"

"Don't worry about it," he said. "You'll be great."

Christian Dramas like these swept the nation during the years I attended high school. Designed to minister to anyone, no matter his or her language or level of IQ, the plays were brief but powerful portraits-in-motion of what it meant to turn from evil and follow Christ. There were no words, only a loud background track where the music was warm and happy when someone accepted Christ into his heart, choppy and discordant if he followed the wayward path of sinners. Sort of like a Looney Tunes sound track. The actors wore black clothing and white face paint. It was all very dramatic.

Now that I think about it, three out of the five parts in that particular Drama were demonic parts, so I shouldn't have felt that Cory was singling me out. Being the lead was out of the question since I'd never acted before, and I certainly didn't envy the person playing the Jesusy figure. Saving humanity from sin and death was much too daunting. I tried to convince Cory that a demon of laziness would have been much more effective and less cliché than a drunken one, but that argument didn't get very far. Had he agreed, I could have slept through the entire Drama. As it was, I'd soon be standing in front of people, pounding invisible beer after invisible beer. I didn't even *like* invisible beer. And though I had no personal experience to draw from, feigning drunkenness seemed infinitely worse than actually getting drunk—you'd remember everything.

Evangelism has never been my favorite part of the faith, at first because I felt embarrassed to accost virtual strangers with pamphlets, tracts, and flyers extolling the love of Christ. It was as if Christ were a kegger I was throwing next weekend or an overpriced cell-phone plan. Ministry tools like the *Jesus* Film, the EvangeCube, and "The Lord's Gym" T-shirts did nothing to make the process more natural. I didn't understand how these props would convince anyone of much else than the fact that Christian marketers and filmmakers needed more training.

I struggled with my aversion to the task that is known among Christians as "sharing the Gospel," "giving your testimony," or "reaching out." Those names overflow with generosity of spirit. The only way we know anything, after all, is because someone along the way has shared, given, reached out. The idea is equally beautiful: "I know Someone wonderful," it says, "and I'd like to introduce you." Stories from the Bible carry that message, too. Jesus invites himself over to the houses of people he meets, breaks bread with them. Drinks wine with them. Hangs out. He talks with them about what's bugging them—maybe it's the leprosy, or the death of a family member. Sometimes it has to do with spiritual clarity or not feeling peaceful. He helps them out, sometimes challenging them with new ideas, sometimes washing their feet, sometimes just sitting with them. "Go forth unto all nations and share the Gospel," he said. But somewhere along the way, we stopped "sharing" and started prepping for debate. In the translation from idea to action, at some point in the decades that piled up between Jesus and me, something got lost.

The outcome of all the sharing, giving, and reaching out, surprisingly, is known today in many Christian circles as "winning people for the Lord." There is a sudden but clear change in metaphors: the message of Christ is no longer a gift to be shared. Instead, it becomes a tool with which to "win" pew fillers. Visions of evangelists in front of giant Risk boards come to mind, each deciding which missionaries to move where in order to achieve total world domination. I can't claim any sort of innocence in all this, except to say that my motives were steeped in compassion. I believed with all my heart that Jesus would change people's lives for the bet-

feigning drunkenness seemed infinitely worse than actually getting drunk—you'd remember everything.

ter. Perhaps I felt like the most idealistic of presidential candidates the night before a big televised debate. I believed in what I was saying, that if everyone else understood what I did, we could save the world. I didn't like the format at all, but that didn't change the fact that I had a strong message.

•   •   •

I tried being a good drunken demon. I timed the opening of each invisible beer with the *pop, fizz!* on the sound track, I contorted my face to a sinister—or at least constipated—grimace, I hit my marks as directed. I was awful. What was worse, my friends had all gotten released of their Dramatic duties on account of their being in the band.

At the end of the week everybody's parents came for an advanced screening of our performance. Though I couldn't see my parents' expressions of sympathetic horror from my mark on the stage, I imagined them. Their attempts to appear encouraging were as transparent as my attempt to appear drunk. Despite all of it, though, they still came up after the performance for hugs and congratulations.

I've wondered if they would still be proud if they had known how disastrous the results of the trip were going to be. The Drama itself was terrible, as was my powerful and moving representation of the demonic. Our foray into acting, however embarrassing it seems now, was not worse than the nights we overheard Mike yelling at Vickie over some unresolved schedule conflict, or how he told us one night we were "the worst bunch of teenagers" he'd ever worked with. It was not worse than the way that the leaders got uncomfortable at any hint of gender closeness they detected—even when they saw Cana massaging her older brother's shoulders one night after a concert. Nor worse than the fact that their hyperprudishness did nothing to deter one girl on the trip from losing her virginity to one of the local boys. My parents weren't proud that I was part of this Youth for Truth team, nor that I'd be passing out flyers in the suburbs of Sydney in a few days. But they were still proud. I could tell by the way they hugged me, by the way they helped me raise money to go, by the way they refrained from pointing out the large and numerous theological holes in the way we were attempting to minister to the world. They saw the best and did not harp on the worst. A Testamint, perhaps, to the grace and patience of a mother. Of a father.

se I liked being with

whirlybirds

For one summer, while I was home from my first year of college, I attended a Charismatic church in town with Cana. It was her church, and I went along because I liked being with her, liked listening to her voice, guttural and strong, singing the worship songs. Cana was always a bigger believer in miracles than I was. She prayed over things, told stories she'd heard of tiny churches in Africa that had raised people from the dead. A few years out of high school, she had a dream in which God told her what she should name her first daughter. Imagine that. I dream of ballroom dancing with Bono at my old elementary school or my teeth falling out after I've eaten a banana. These scenarios don't seem to have much significance, spiritual or otherwise, so I don't tend to pay much attention anymore. Although I do sometimes avoid bananas.

It wasn't that I didn't want to believe in miracles. The opposite was true. I was, perhaps still am, intensely jealous that Cana could hear God this way. Once, I tried very hard to help cast out a demon. I didn't do the actual praying, just held out my hands while someone else prayed fervently that the demon who was setting up shop in so-and-so's mind would kindly LEAVE, IN THE NAME OF JESUS! Nothing happened. But we prayed for upwards of an hour. I remember sweating a lot and begging God silently to please do something. I wanted to see the demon leave. Perhaps he would shrivel as his weak little spirit left, wafting and translucent like the scents of freshly baked pies in old cartoons. We saw no such thing, but the boy claimed to feel better once we were finished. This did not seem at all miraculous to me, as I'm sure the boy was only feeling better because the long, sweaty prayer was over.

Cana's church met in a giant temporary tent. Their old building was being torn down to make room for the newer, more modern, and definitely more massive sanctuary that they'd need to hold the growing number of congregants who called the church their home. The tent was actually comfortable, with its makeshift stage and makeshift lighting, its speakers, projectors, microphones, plush carpeting. None of it seemed makeshift at all.

this did not seem at all miraculous to me, as i'm sure the boy was only feeling better because the long, sweaty prayer was over.

I tried to get over the bombastic pastor. With his Burt Reynolds mustache, mock turtlenecks, and emphasis on exclamatory sentences, he reminded me more of a car salesman than a pastor. Plus, my dad had coached Little League with him a few years back and used to complain about how every year Norman loaded his team with the best players and the richest team moms with the tastiest snacks. He was the George Steinbrenner of the local YMCA. To his credit, Norman's theology and his coaching philosophy did not conflict—he advocated, each Sunday, that God wanted only the best for your life: the kindest spouse, the most lucrative job, a top-of-the-line sanctuary, the best shortstop. Although my dad and his losing teams didn't agree, it was no wonder Norman's church was growing so rapidly. People loved hearing that God wanted to bless their every endeavor. I know I did. And if Norman's life was any indication of the truth of his message, every word

people loved hearing that god wanted to bless their every endeavor. i know i did.

he said was true. His new car in the parking lot and his fancy microphones onstage were evidence.

The mood, one Sunday, was more emotive than usual. The music had more key changes than were necessary and Norman's exclamatory sentences were enunciated with a vigor that made him nearly bounce down the aisles. He was pointing to people in the congregation, calling worshippers to approach the stage for healing and encouragement. Then, one by one, as Pastor Norman was praying, each person would crumple to the ground: "slain in the Spirit," they call it. A spotter walked around with the pastor to make sure no one would accidentally "get a concussion from the Spirit."

I wasn't sure what to think about all this.

On one hand, I had never been slain in the Spirit before, and I was curious. (The only time I had fainted at all was during a party when one of my friends introduced us to the idea of passing out for fun by putting pressure on the neck to slow blood flow to the brain. It was not a particularly enlightening experience, but losing consciousness was weirdly thrilling for a bunch of kids who'd never touched anything like hallucinogens or alcohol, and each of us woke up seconds later completely disoriented and feeling as though we'd slept all night. I've since learned that one can die from this. And understanding what I do now about blood flow and how necessary it is for the brain and, you know, its brainly activity, I'm not really surprised.) I believed in the miraculous the same way I believed in Europe: I'd heard of it, I knew it existed, and it would be really nice to get a firsthand glimpse. So I prayed with one half of my heart that Norman would shoot that pointer finger in my direction.

On the other hand, I was completely mortified at the thought of getting up in front of all those people and not getting slain in the Spirit, and I was pretty certain that would be the way it would go down. It would be like the spelling bee of religious experiences: spelling the word *then* with an *a* instead of an *e,* waiting for the look of disappointment to wash across the teacher's face, knowing that your classmates now realize how subpar you really are. Bastards. So the other half of my heart prayed that Norman would point to anyone but me. I was content to remain unnoticed and unmiraculous.

I am one in a somewhat narrow segment of society who can say she has believed in God for as long as she can remember. This was sort of discouraging as a teenager, especially when it came time for Sharing Your Testimony. My story was always less glamorous than my friends', and it usually went something like this: "I was raised Christian and I asked Jesus into my heart when I was about five." (Although there is a story about my actual moment of conversion, I do not remember the exact age of the occurrence. Rather, I tend to label everything that happened in my first-remembered life as happening at the age of five. It was a busy year.) I would recount this testimony as quickly as possible, almost apologetically, so that those with the more dramatic stories could speak. Stories of preconversion drugs, fornication, and partying were much more compelling and, somehow, more Christian than my own boring tale. Jesus was always involved in thrilling, theatrical conversions of the most wayward sinners. And although I don't remember any biblical conversion stories being about potheads, I do remember tax collectors and Pharisees, whose sins, according to my Sunday School teachers, on the scale of "Just How Bad Is That?" were about equivalent.

People told me not to be embarrassed that I didn't have a more interesting conversion. It was miracle enough that I had been a Christian my whole life, they said. But I knew they were just trying to be nice. Being a Christian your whole life is like inheriting wealth: you don't really deserve it, you're just benefiting from your parents' decisions. I wanted God to do something truly miraculous so I could have a better story. I contemplated becoming a nonbeliever for a while so that I could be wide open and available for something more God-inspired to happen. I would do as Briony did in Ian McEwan's *Atonement:* "wait on the bridge, calm and obstinate, until events, real events, not her own fantasies, rose to her challenge, and dispelled her insignificance."[1] This sounded good. I would just wait until a miracle happened. I believed it would. I really,

really, really wanted it to. Was desperate for it, even. So, in the meantime, I would wait on the bridge.

I can't help but believe that God must get a little laugh at our definition of *miracle: miracle* (n.): "A marvellous event not ascribable to human power or the operation of any natural force and therefore attributed to supernatural, esp. divine, agency; *esp.* an act (e.g. of healing) demonstrating control over nature and serving as evidence that the agent is either divine or divinely favoured."[2]

Those of us who believe in God presumably attribute all things—natural, scientific, explainable, unexplainable—to supernatural, esp. divine, agency. The miraculous, then, becomes simply "something we're not used to." As my dad often argues, "If I could go back in time to Jesus' day and bring a flashlight, the flashlight would be the miracle."

there was no precedent for remaining standing, and i wasn't sure i was a good enough actress to fake falling down.

When Pastor Norman did finally point in my direction, my knees were wobbly and I wasn't sure that I would make it all the way to the front of the tent. I cannot remember if he prayed in tongues or in English (I was too distracted with willing myself to be slain in the Spirit to pay attention to minutiae like that). I do know he prayed long enough that I got to wondering how long I should let him go before it would all begin to seem silly to him and the rest of the congregation, who, I'm sure, were waiting for their turn to be pointed at.

My friend Maria was in a similar situation once at a religious summer camp. Everybody was laying hands on her, praying for her to get the gift of tongues. So she did. She made up tongues: a bunch of garbled half syllables that increased gradually in volume. And the people rejoiced, called her mother, rejoiced some more. They left that day with their faith renewed; Maria left with faith somewhat less so.

I wondered how I would end my own public prayer session. Or even if I could end it. Everyone else had fallen over, so there was no precedent for remaining standing, and I wasn't sure I was a good enough actress to fake falling down. I was scared of bruising something. I'd have to improvise. So I reached over, mid-prayer, and hugged Pastor Norman as if he'd just rescued me from the *Titanic*.

Hmm . . .

I realized almost immediately that it was the wrong thing to do. Perhaps it was the bewildered and slightly offended look he gave me when I pulled away, like he wanted everyone to know that he was not one of those pervy pastors who enjoyed being hugged by minors, that it just sort of happened to him and he was not soliciting the scandalous embrace in any way—after all, didn't everyone see the way he kept his hands to himself? How he didn't hug me back or even slightly reciprocate the gesture? In any case, I wandered back to my seat and watched as more people fell over. I felt my face get hot with embarrassment and hoped that the shame was misinterpreted as holy joy.

Scott and I recently watched a documentary titled *Hands on a Hard Body* about a radio contest where people compete for a brand-new truck. (As my friend Laura says, it is not nearly as sexy as it sounds. But nothing ever is.) The person who can stand next to the truck longest, one hand on its hard body, in the heat of a hot Texas sun, wins it. Scott and I both tried to predict who would win. I had my money on a woman with no front teeth. She seemed like she needed the truck most, and she was prepared, too: before the contest, she went for weeks without air-conditioning so her body would acclimate to the intense heat of the outdoors. This may not seem to be a big deal, but she and her husband were accustomed to living in a tiny trailer that was jerry-rigged with an air conditioner that had formerly been used to cool an entire Kmart. So you can see she was dedicated. But even though she probably needed that truck more than anyone else did, the woman lost after many hours into the contest because she felt the judges were being unfair. She lost because she got irritated and angry; in her desperation, she let her emotions take over and she decided to walk away.

There is certainly a reason that the word *desperation* has so many negative connotations associated with it—Gatsby and his notorious green light could tell you that much. I used to think that I would acquire spiritual gifts—the gift of tongues or prophetic dreams—if I wanted them badly enough. Jesus said that even tiny, measly mustard-seed faith could move a mountain. I wanted something far smaller, but even when I put all of my faith together, it was not measly enough to do something even slightly miraculous. I prayed for it, I reassured God that I believed in Him and His power to move even large landmasses, I went to church, and I grew more and more despondent. My faith in God wavered slightly, but it was my faith in my own faith that took the largest hit. Did I have less faith than virtually everyone else in that temporary church tent? Was everyone else wanting more, praying better, submitting more trustingly than I was?

It would be easier to dismiss miracles completely if there wasn't so much emphasis on them in the Bible, especially in the Gospels and Acts. I tend to dismiss a lot of things because I'm not good at them, like athletics, or because I feel like they don't really apply to me, like some speed limits. But no matter how I feel about miracles, or how many television healers are called out as fakes, or how many people I pray for who don't get miraculously healed or saved or surprised with huge sums of money, I can't get around the fact that Jesus said: "These signs will accompany those who have believed: in My name they will cast out demons, they will speak with new tongues; they will pick up serpents, and if they drink any deadly poison, it will not hurt them; they will lay hands on the sick, and they will recover." And he said this to the disciples right before he was to leave them for good, so it seems like he might have put a little thought into it. The section of Mark in which this charge appears is considered somewhat problematic by scholars, and a lot of smart thinkers have a lot to say about what this might mean for modern-day people who aren't poison drinkers or snake handlers; but if you judged my life on whether or not I was doing any of these things, I would be in the same place I was in the first-grade spelling bee: out.

even when i put all of my faith together, it was not measly enough to do something even slightly miraculous.

I spoke to my pastor, Tim, about the issue. Tim is—and I think he'll forgive me for saying this—about as unmiraculous as I am (his conversion story is, too), but he's also one of the most faithful people I know. He said he thought it was unfair to compare what miracles we see today on television to the miracles that Jesus was doing. Jesus wasn't doing magic shows, he said, but rather working to "put the world to rights." I thought about one healer that my husband always yells at when he comes on TV, a guy with a very bad hairpiece and pants that never fit, although these fashion missteps are not usually why Scott is so mad. This particular healer behaves much like a street-corner magician, asking the audience questions like, "Is there any way I could have known this?" and "Have you told anyone here today about your condition?" It's as if he's trying to prove his otherworldly powers, and I half expect there to be a rabbit involved. I get embarrassed that guys like him are "on my team," so to speak, and even though I know I shouldn't judge them, I sometimes can't help thinking what faking fakers they are and how God is someday going to tell them where they can put all their false promises and bags of stolen money. But, like I said, I shouldn't judge.

"peter is healed," he said. "we just won't see it until we meet jesus."

A family I used to attend church with has two of three children diagnosed with a rare disease that makes their bodies reject food as it would an infection. The younger child, Peter, only three when he was diagnosed, is hooked to feeding tubes that send a special amino-acid-based formula into his system to keep him nourished and alive. He throws up almost immediately if he tries to ingest any kind of food at all—it doesn't matter how much or what kind; any food is treated as an invader. He's left with only an intravenous meal and some cubes of ice to munch on as the rest of the family sits around the table for dinner.

Peter's dad said that he once got a call from a friend saying that he'd been praying and that God, in no uncertain terms, told him Peter was healed. This friend had something of a record when it came to miraculous healings—apparently, he was the conduit God used to send messages. When Peter's dad told me the story, though, it was obvious that Peter was not better. His dad's eyes looked tired, his voice sounded flat— these were signs of a caretaker who has been at work awhile. A man who has waited on a miracle for a long time. I expected him to show a little anger. What kind of friend calls up with a message like that when he hasn't been there, adjusting feeding tubes or measuring out medicine? His response surprised me: "Peter *is* healed," he said. "We just won't see it until we meet Jesus."

That kind of faith eludes me. Although I scoff at people who treat God as a candy dispenser who should pop out a gumball whenever they decide to ask for one, I do it, too. My father-in-law, Rick, was recently diagnosed with cancer, and the only way I can pray is to ask for complete healing: the kind I can see now—not later. I can't quite bring myself to trust God totally, to know that His answer is best even if it's not the miracle I want. I keep trying to think of phrases that will clinch the deal. I want to con God into giving me my gumball.

It's safe to say that my approach is somewhat shortsighted in light of eternity. If I say I believe in forever, in a heaven where all things become right and good, then I suppose I should act like it. I suppose I should stop pretending that God's refusal to grant my every wish is also him refusing to answer my prayers. Answers, after all, aren't always "yes." I should be grateful that he doesn't grant my every request. And a God who heals the people who have the *most* praying friends isn't really my kind of God, anyway. But I also believe that God is patient with me, that He listens to my honest and most heartfelt prayers (even those that are theologically incorrect), and that He yearns for our wholeness. He sees eternity more easily than I do: "My thoughts are not your thoughts," He said. And I remember how arrogant it is for me to order God around on all my little errands, having small crises of faith every time I don't get what I've asked for.

Perhaps the best approach to the miraculous is with a very wide net—a loose interpretation of whatever definition of *miracle* is currently in theological vogue, a desire to watch for God's hand at work, to err on the side of overdesignating miracles rather than missing them completely. A generous acceptance of miracles seems better than manipulating them, faking them, pining for, or forcing them. Maybe we should trust a bit more and pay more attention.

i suppose i should stop pretending that god's refusal to grant my every wish is also him refusing to answer my prayers.

Peter's dad tells the story of the first night his family was home after Peter's diagnosis. He and his wife struggled when it came time to prepare dinner for the rest of the family, but they knew the whole family couldn't stop eating. Peter sat on the couch with a cupful of ice as one of his sisters set the table, as his mother browned some ground beef for tacos, as the smell of chopped onions wafted in from the kitchen. Their hearts were breaking because their son would never be able to enjoy the taste of food again. All of them, in the midst of the preparation, were realizing it. But in the midst of his heartbreak, Peter's father glanced up from his onions to see his three kids, in a row on the couch, each munching from his or her own cup of ice. For a moment, the world was right.

today, the whirlybirds were not weeds but hundreds of twirling white raindrops.

Miles and I sat on the porch this spring and watched the whirlybirds fall from our neighbor's tree. I thought about how I would soon grow irritated at the number of whirlybirds that would collect on my porch, the windshield of my car, the crevices of the flower beds, the pot of my tomato plant. I knew that many of the whirlybirds would take root in the soil I'd just finished weeding—they'd reach down, break free of their skins, burst green roots, and sprout pointy leaves. I'd yank them up, one by one, preventing them from overtaking the yard that my husband and I spend just enough time on to keep it from becoming a condemned area. But today, the whirlybirds were not weeds but hundreds of twirling white raindrops, and the tiny clicks they made upon landing on the driveway mesmerized my eight-month-old son and me both. I picked one up for

Miles to examine. I made whirling sounds as he fingered the tiny seed, bringing his eyebrows together in concentration and pointing quizzically at the delicate wing. There would only be a day or two of this scattering as the trees sent out the flying seeds in all directions; then the gathering up would ensue.

I was reminded of what Frederick Buechner calls the "clack-clack" and what Dostoyevsky means when he writes of "sticky green leaves"—the natural world breaking in every once in a while to remind us of God's mercies. This is a miracle. It may not be enough of a miracle for some people, and it wouldn't have been enough of a miracle for the girl I used to be, the girl who wanted to cast out demons and be slain in the Spirit. But now this sort of quiet, whimsical miracle might appeal to me even more than the louder kind. I whispered a tiny prayer of thanks between the whirls, whispered it into my son's ear so he might remember, too.

Acknowledgments

I acknowledge that my family has been very gracious in letting me tell our stories, in whatever incomplete way that I have. Scott, Miles, Genevieve, Dad, Mom, Hutch, Kristina, Rick, Vonnie, Johnson clan: I love you. Thank you for being my favorite subjects, readers, and cheerleaders. Oh, and Kristina, just because you didn't appear in the text of this book doesn't mean you're off the hook. It just means I'm saving a good Costa Rica story for next time.

I acknowledge that I have stolen ideas from a lot of good pastors. This is, actually, the secret to writing a book on faith. There. I told you. Here are the recent pastors who have, wittingly or not, given me some wonderful material, both in their sermons and in the way that they live: Mindy and Josh Hancock, Tim Suttle, Scott Savage, and Rick Savage.

I acknowledge that I subjected many people to reading early, "shitty first drafts" of these stories. Thank you for being kinder than you should have been. Kristin Suttle was one of the first people I felt brave enough to show the finished product to. My friend and colleague Maria Polonchek has read every last word and has painstakingly helped me shape this manuscript through every step of the process. Thanks for helping me move my Post-its over.

I acknowledge that I have sat in the classrooms of many teachers who have helped me begin to love language and learning. Here's a list of just a few who were so important to me: Mr. Leonard, Mrs. Smith, Mrs. Allison, Mrs. Foutz, Mr. Graham, Mr. Herold, Mr. Miller, Mr. Rossi, Dr. McKinney, Dean Nelson, Dr. Martin, the adjunct speech teacher (whose name I can't remember!) who wrote on one of my homework papers *You are a good writer! You should think about using this skill in a future career*, Mike Johnson, Dr. Atkins, Laura Moriarty.

I acknowledge that I have been lucky to work with people who are encouraging, smart, kind, and able to deal with minor freak-outs and stupid questions. Philis Boultinghouse, Amanda Demastus, and the team at Howard Books; Margaret Riley and Jennifer Rudolph Walsh at WME: How can I thank you for giving me a shot? I feel more than lucky.

In a writing workshop once, a girl who often wore sweatshirts with cats on them and her hair in braid-buns wrote on one of my papers: *What denomination ARE you?!?* The question made me laugh. I suppose it was funny because the denomination I claim seems so unimportant in the scope of Christian history. I'm at a place where I enjoy borrowing ideas and practices and bits of dogma from a number of different traditions and I relate well to any denomination that claims "Jesus is Lord!" So the thing I want to acknowledge is this: Thank you to the Church Universal, the diversity with which you worship, the numerous ways in which you seek to encounter the living God, the nuances of your worship services—the ones I understand and the ones I don't, the ones I agree with and the ones I don't, the ones I admire and the ones I participate in. And thank you to cat sweatshirt girl for helping bring this gratitude to my attention.

Finally, I acknowledge that my God is very, very good and able to do more than we can ever ask or imagine. Thank You for being so utterly worthy. You are pretty cool.

Notes

INTRODUCTION

1. Anne Lamott. *Traveling Mercies: Some Thoughts on Faith.* New York: Pantheon, 1999, 128.

2. Flannery O'Connor. *Mystery and Manners: Occasional Prose.* New York: Farrar, Straus and Giroux, 1969, 150.

WHAT TO EXPECT WHEN (YOU HAVE NO IDEA WHAT) YOU ARE EXPECTING

1. Genesis 1:2. Translation by Martin Buber and Franz Rosenzweig. Translated by Lawrence Rosenwald with Everett Fox. Indianapolis: Indiana University Press, 1994; "People Today and the Jewish Bible: From a Lecture Series" by Martin Buber (November 1926).

2. Daniel Taylor. *The Myth of Certainty: The Reflective Christian and the Risk of Commitment.* Westmont, IL: InterVarsity, 1999, 81.

3. Richard Rohr. *The Naked Now: Learning to See as the Mystics See.* New York: Crossroad, 2009, 25–26.

223

MAKING SPACE

1. Buechner, Frederick. *Listening to Your Life: Daily Meditations*. San Francisco: Harper, 1992, 339.

2. Ibid., 78.

HOW TO PLAY

1. Clifford Geertz. *The Interpretation of Cultures*. New York: Basic Books, 1973.

2. Robert Benson. From a sermon titled "The Echo Within" at Redemption Church, Olathe, KS, July 11, 2010.

3. Robert Benson. From a sermon titled "The Echo Within" at Redemption Church, Olathe, KS, July 11, 2010.

4. Martin Buber. *I and Thou*. New York: Charles Scribner's Sons, 1970, 80.

5. Eugene H. Peterson. *Practice Resurrection: A Conversation on Growing Up in Christ*. Grand Rapids, MI: Eerdmans, 2010, 167.

6. Ibid., 37.

THE SECOND WEEK

1. Jay C. Rochelle. "Beginnings and Ends (The Spirituality of Advent, Christmas, and Epiphany)." *Currents in Theology and Mission* 9:6D (1982), 325.

2. Wendell Berry. *The Way of Ignorance*. Berkeley, CA: Shoemaker & Hoard, 2005, 107–108.

3. Annie Dillard. *The Writing Life*. New York: Harper & Row, 1989, 32.

4. Lamott, 95.

NOTES

GETTING IT OUT

1. Rainer Maria Rilke. *Rilke's Book of Hours*. Translated by Anita Barrows and Joanna Macy. New York: Riverhead, 1996, 55.

BUT DAIRY COWS ALREADY KNEW THIS

1. Alexander Schmemann. *For the Life of the World*. Yonkers, NY: St. Vladimir's Seminary Press, 1973, 35.

2. Sara Miles. *Take This Bread*. New York: Ballantine, 2007, 49.

A SPRINKLING

1. Lamott, 231–232.

2. N. T. Wright. *Surprised by Hope: Rethinking Heaven, the Resurrection, and the Mission of the Church*. New York: HarperOne, 2008, 271.

3. Ibid., 272.

4. Definition comes from Dictionary.com.

5. Wright, p. 259.

6. Marilynne Robinson. *Gilead*. New York: Picador, 2006, 31.

THE PREACHER'S WIFE

1. Dorothy Harrison Pentecost. *The Pastor's Wife and the Church*. Chicago: Moody, 1964, 154–155.

2. Ibid., 144.

3. Ibid., 145.

WHIRLYBIRDS

1. Ian McEwan. *Atonement*. New York: Anchor, 2001, 98.

2. Definition comes from the *Oxford English Dictionary*, online database.

Grace in the Maybe

Katie Savage

Reading Group Guide

INTRODUCTION

For many people, going to church is routine, much like going to school or work, and often it seemingly has no connection with the other six days of the week or "real life." In *Grace in the Maybe,* Katie Savage connects the reality (and humor) of her life with the seasons of the church calendar and reflects on how these seasons provide a big-picture framework for living each day. Whether readers have grown up in a liturgical tradition or not, *Grace in the Maybe* is a collection of delightful personal reflections on the intersection of real life and faith.

TOPICS & QUESTIONS FOR DISCUSSION

1. Did you grow up in a faith tradition that was ordered around the liturgical church calendar? If so, how did it impact you? If not, what is your initial response to reading about life within the church calendar?

2. Do you relate more to a faith rooted in certainty or mystery? Describe which factors and influences in your life have contributed to your preference.

3. Read the announcement of Jesus' birth to Mary in Luke 2:26–38 and the subsequent appearance to Joseph in Matthew 1:18–25. How do surprise and doubt factor into the season of Advent based upon these stories of the first Advent? What surprises or doubts have you encountered on your journey of faith and how have you responded to them?

4. In Chapter 2 ("Leaning In"), the author describes Christmas as "the culmination of the Christian season of Advent." How does this view of Christmas differ from cultural and even many "Christian" views of Christmas? Has reading about Advent spurred your imagination to engage with the season differently this year? Describe.

5. What are your favorite kinds of gifts to receive? On page 42, the author says: "The gift of Jesus is so personal that it cuts to the very interior of our hearts....We are known."

How does this description of Jesus compare to your experience with Him? How does it impact you when you reflect on being known by Jesus?

6. Reflect on a favorite memory of time spent with friends or family. How does this kind of time connect with your experience of church? How does the author's definition of church on page 76—"His people, living life alongside one another, giving the best of themselves to each other and to God as often as they can"—challenge and/or inspire you?

7. When you hear the word *Lent* what is the first thing that comes to your mind? How does this compare with the author's reflections on Lent?

8. In Chapter 6 ("The Second Week"), the author discusses the gift of seasons. She says, "In the deepest parts of our souls, I think, we long for seasons." (page 91) Is this true for you? Why or why not? Drawing upon the metaphor of seasons in the year, how would you describe the current season of your life with God?

9. On pages 89 and 90, the author reflects on spring flowers following a hard winter: "new life looks much better after a cold, hard, long bout with death and freeze." Has there been a time in your life when you experienced "new life" after a difficult season? What sustained you during the difficult season?

10. Did you grow up with a view of life being more like a straight line up (i.e., one "graduation" after another) or a collection of seasons and cycles? How has your perspective

(linear or cyclical) impacted how you respond to the reality of everyday life?

11. Do you agree with the author's comment that our culture is drawn to seasonless living? What are some of the visible "unnatural measures we go through to make sure we're always comfortable"(page 91)? What are the ways that trying to live a seasonless life is costly to our humanity?

12. What do you think is the purpose of a season (like Lent or Advent) that is focused on reflecting on sin and repentance? What is the role of confession of sin in your faith tradition? Read Luke 15:11–24. What does this parable say about God's heart toward us when we sin? How does this affect how you see yourself when you fail or sin?

13. On page 143, the author writes: "our primary human longing is for nearness—to each other and to God." Do you relate to this longing? How does the notion of being dependent on God and living in community with people impact you? What is the difference between codependence and interdependence? In what ways have you experienced the gifts of living in dependence on God and in community with others?

14. The author quotes Orthodox theologian Alexander Schmemann who said: "Man is a sacrificial being because he finds his life in love, and love is sacrificial" (pages 126 and 127) Have you ever been the recipient of someone else's sacrifice on your behalf? How did it impact you? For what are you willing to sacrifice your time, money, or energy?

15. What are some of your favorite Easter traditions? How would you describe the good news of Easter? How is the symbol of baptism related to the good news of Easter? What do you think would be necessary for Easter to be more celebrated?

16. Do you identify with the author's reflection on page 156: "The problem is no longer that we merely love our stuff, but that we find our meaning in it, our being"? What "things" or "stuff" are you tempted to trust instead of God? What is the difference between *enjoying* the "things" in our life and *trusting* them?

17. Does it surprise you to know that the word *nice* isn't used anywhere in most translations of the Bible? Jesus sums up the Law and the Prophets with the greatest commandment: "Love the Lord your God with all your heart and with all your soul and with all your mind....Love your neighbor as yourself." (Matthew 22:36–40) How does love contrast with niceness?

18. In the last chapter, the author discusses watching whirly-birds fall from trees and describes the experience as a miracle. How does this use of the word *miracle* impact you? From this perspective, think about some of the miracles in your life each day. How could this perspective transform "ordinary time"?

ENHANCE YOUR BOOK CLUB

1. Pick one season from the church calendar and do some research on the historical practices or feasts observed during this season. Discuss what you learned about the season during your book club meetings and consider collectively implementing some of the practices or observances this year during the season.

2. Consider attending a liturgical church service as a group. Pay attention to the visual symbols and physical movement throughout the service. Notice how you are impacted by the various parts of the service and take note of what aspects either draw you closer or move you away from connecting with God. Go to lunch afterward to discuss your various experiences.

3. A related practice to the liturgical church calendar is liturgical prayer. Select a prayer book like *The Book of Common Prayer, The Divine Hours,* or the *Celtic Daily Prayer* and use it to "pray the hours" or choose one of the prayer times each day for one month. Discuss your experience with this way of praying at your next book club.

A CONVERSATION WITH KATIE SAVAGE

What was the inspiration for writing this book?

In my very first graduate writing course I wanted to write about the experience with the chin whisker—it was a funny story, but for me it needed to be more than that; so for a very long time I thought about how the story might be significant. The church I was attending at the time was pretty faithful to the liturgical readings, and since it was the first time I had participated in using the church calendar, I was very interested to learn as much as I could. Somehow, the whisker and the church calendar were mingling together in my mind. (Is it weird that a whisker was the inspiration for this book? I know what you're thinking: "Absolutely. Yes.") I remember talking to my friend Emily during our hour-long commute to school about how I wanted to do a whole book of essays about Advent. So it began there, but it was a tad limiting to write within only one season, so I expanded it.

When did you first encounter the liturgical church calendar? Do you have a favorite season? If so, what makes it your favorite?

I've gotten familiar with the church calendar only recently—maybe within the past five years. But even though I couldn't necessarily name the church seasons or tell you much about them, belonging to the church for so long has helped me feel that

I've been *experiencing* the seasons my whole life. Last year, my cousin Ayme said that she'd decided to celebrate Advent with her family for the first time and was looking for ideas about how to do that. I told her she'd been celebrating Advent for years— she was teaching her boys the stories and living in the reality of what Jesus' birth meant. Maybe she was naming it for the first time, like I have been, but that's only secondary to knowing deep within yourself the truth behind each of these seasons.

My favorite season changes all the time. I can't choose just one. It's like asking if I like *Billy Madison* or *Shakespeare in Love* better. I can't choose! They're both favorites. (Sorry that you now know about my somewhat questionable taste in movies. But I would rather watch Adam Sandler draw a blue duck fifty times than pop in *The Godfather.* It is a character flaw. I know.) I will tell you that I'm generally more drawn to the seasons in which we're to celebrate: Easter, Christmas.

You talk about the expectations often placed on preacher's wives. What practices or guidance have been influential in helping you maintain your own identity, apart from your role as the wife of a pastor?

My mother-in-law is a great example of what a pastor's wife should be. I just try to do whatever she does—although I never sing "specials," which I'm sure my church appreciates. I also owe a great debt to my parents for never letting me believe there was something I couldn't do. They sometimes balk at the word *feminist*, but they raised me in such a way that I never felt constrained by gender expectations.

Beyond that, I think I have begun to feel comfortable in a very honest sort of faith. By that I mean that I know I've written things and feel things and do things that other people will disagree with. Sometimes they will disagree with me because they don't think the ideas or the actions or the feelings are holy enough. Lots of times, they will be right. But I don't think it helps anyone to pretend that we don't all struggle with how to live up to the name "Christian." It's unhelpful. I have learned the most about how to better love God and humanity from people who try to live transparently and humbly. Even (or perhaps especially) in positions of prominence in the church.

***Grace in the Maybe* is a collection of stories, and at various points throughout the book you talk about the importance of storytelling. What have been some significant influences in your formation as a storyteller?**

We are all storytellers. I just happen to write mine down because telling them to actual people who are actually listening to me actually move my mouth is not really my thing. My comedic timing and sense of detail and pace are much better when I get weeks to agonize over it all.

That being said, I think there have been a few people who have strongly influenced the way I think about the art of story. When I first read Anne Lamott, for instance, I felt this incredible light-bulb moment. This was a way that I could talk about God, which is something I've felt called to do for a very long time. It's in a style that is not necessarily formal or trained. It's definitely not platitude-filled or false sounding. It's brave and deep and pulled from experiences that are so *normal*.

One of my first writing teachers, Dean Nelson, once said this (well, probably more than once): "Nothing kills your writing faster than thinking you're writing big, grand ideas. Just tell the story."

Scott's grandpa was a wonderful storyteller, too. He was a preacher, and during his "retirement years" he filled the pulpit at many different churches in California. After he died, we found a little book with a list of what stories he told when to which congregations. He didn't want to retell a story he'd already used—even though he never had the same respect for his family. We heard the same family stories over and over and over. I loved his repertoire of stories. Everybody knew which story he was about to start in on. Nobody, not even his wife, tired of hearing them. He showed me what the Scriptures must have been like for your average ancient Israelite: Nothing to read, just stories to tell and retell, to love and hold in your heart, to help you understand God.

How did you make the shift from high school teacher to author? Do you miss anything about being in the classroom?

Oh, yes. I miss the classroom. My first year, I taught seventh-grade English. Most people say something along the lines of "Bless your heart" when they hear that, but it was so rewarding. Middle-school kids are crazy cool—they are funny without meaning to be; they still think their teachers know something; they let you mold their ideas about literature and life a little.

Sometimes they smell bad because they haven't yet figured out the benefits of deodorant, but that's a small thing.

The transition to writing as a career (it still feels strange writing that!) did come at a perfect time for me, though. Miles and Genevieve are so young—I love not having to teach during these years. Teaching English is more than a full-time job—it is a lifestyle. If you've never done it, you don't realize how much time and energy grading essays and planning lessons takes. (I don't miss grading essays, by the way. Not ever.) I feel very lucky to have gotten to teach and I feel very lucky to have gotten to write.

You talk about life as a mom in various places throughout the book. Has becoming a mother impacted your life with God and your writing? If so, how?

Motherhood has taught me how difficult it is to love someone well. The kind of love that sacrifices everything: the last bite of ice cream, the morning shower, the time to yourself, the sanity during grocery shopping, the safety and well-being of yourself above anyone else, the pride that comes with being able to "handle" everything. I would do anything for my kids—I feel that in the deepest parts of my soul. And yet, I come so short of loving my kids perfectly. I do things wrong daily. It makes me so grateful to know that God loves me perfectly. And them perfectly. It is a wonderful gift to be able to realize that in a new way.

As far as writing, that's sort of a double-edged sword. Miles and Genevieve give me tons and tons of material—they have helped give me another perspective with which to look at life and God. But they also give me very little time to actually write that material down. So I've had to learn to "protect," as they say, the writing time. I'm not very good at that.

There seems to be a movement among the current generation toward liturgical church traditions. What factors do you think are influencing this trend?

While I can't speak for the whole generation, for me the liturgical church traditions offer a sense of structure that I love. I mean, I enjoy the willy-nilly on occasion and I enjoy babbling to God in whatever honest, free way that I want to pray some days. Other days, however, I find that I don't have the words, or maybe the energy to find the words, to say to God what I am feeling. *The Book of Common Prayer* does. The church seasons help me contemplate different aspects of Christ's life, they challenge me to reflect on sorrow and repentance as much as victory and gladness, they give me the gift of movement when I feel stuck. There's also the added bonus of solidarity with other Christians of all sorts of backgrounds from all different time periods. There's room for these practices in my faith journey, and I like learning from all sorts of denominations of Christians.

When did you begin to know that you were a writer? What do you enjoy most about the writing process? Is there anything you don't enjoy?

I think I have known my whole life. In fifth grade or so, I decided to write a novel on our family's first computer. It was a terrible story. Really, really bad. I still remember the first line, of which I was quite proud: "Maxine walked slowly in her big, bulky jacket." I don't know why I was so proud of that line, but every time I read it over, I thought, *This is going to be so good!* I got eleven pages in—it seemed like a huge accomplishment, like I'd just written *War and Peace*. I never finished it and never let anyone read it, I don't think. (Although I did print out one copy for myself, so it's highly likely that at least one of my parents saw it.) Since then, I always had, in the back of my mind, the dream of writing for a living.

I pursued it quietly, doing a complex little dance of avoidance, not even really admitting it to myself because that would be scary. I majored in English education in college….and then decided to add another major in creative writing. But just because I liked it, not because it was practical. A few years later, I went to graduate school in English literature and had to be almost forced by my friend Maria to sign up for a writing workshop. I wasn't brave enough to do that on my own and I owe her a lot for helping me sign up for that class, then for encouraging me to change my course and get my MFA. I still get very nervous showing someone my work. So you can bet the publishing process has been a bit of a roller coaster of emotions for me.

The thing I love most about writing is most certainly *having written*. The process is difficult, and I try to avoid difficult things whenever possible. I hate how difficult it is coming up with an idea. I hate feeling stuck and watching that damn cursor just blink and blink and blink at me. I hate the perfectionist streak in me that makes each paragraph take agonizingly long to get "just right." I hate that things are usually not "just right" enough. But there is a moment within each essay or chapter when something clicks, and I realize I might actually have something important to say. That moment makes all the rest of it worth it. So the longer I do this, the more I'm learning to trust that that moment will, eventually, after approximately 1,809,111 cursor blinks, happen.

What is one of the main things you hope readers take away from *Grace in the Maybe*?

A deeper love for God. A deeper sense of grace for ourselves and one another. What a gift, if I'm able to be even a small part of making that happen.

Who are some of your favorite authors?

Anne Lamott, Marilynne Robinson, Flannery O'Connor, Ian McEwan, Ralph Ellison, F. Scott Fitzgerald, Frederick Buechner, Fyodor Dostoyevsky.

Now that *Grace in the Maybe* is completed, do you have plans for another book?

I do. But I'm also still swept up in the whirlwind of having *this* book published, so I haven't really been working on anything new as I should be. I also feel as if I might have told all my good stories already. Damn. What if I did that? (Of course that's a big lie, but it's a lie I tend to believe on some days.) Grace for creating new stories, I suppose!